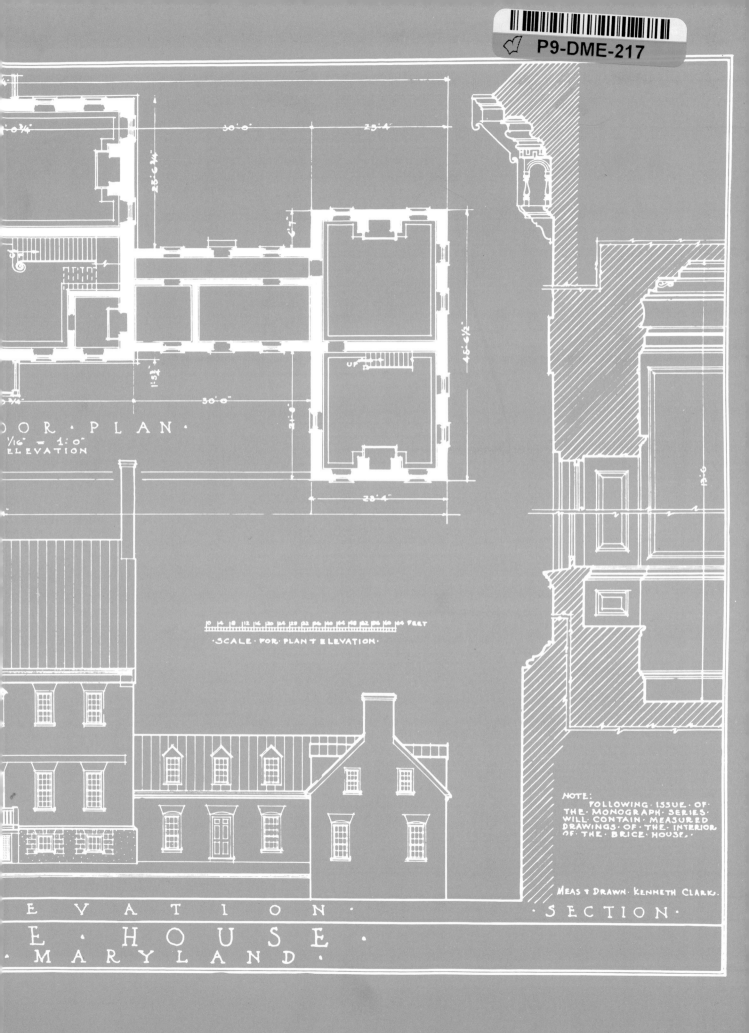

·OOR · P L A N ·
1/16" = 1:0"
ELEVATION

·SCALE · FOR · PLAN ? ELEVATION ·

NOTE:
FOLLOWING · ISSUE · OF ·
THE · MONOGRAPH · SERIES ·
WILL · CONTAIN · MEASURED ·
DRAWINGS · OF · THE · INTERIOR ·
OF · THE · BRICE · HOUSE ·

MEAS ? DRAWN · KENNETH CLARK ·

· E V A T I O N ·   · S E C T I O N ·

· E · H O U S E ·

· M A R Y L A N D ·

NEW ENGLAND BY THE SEA

Other National Historical Society Publications:

THE IMAGE OF WAR: 1861–1865

TOUCHED BY FIRE: A PHOTOGRAPHIC PORTRAIT OF THE CIVIL WAR

WAR OF THE REBELLION: OFFICIAL RECORDS
 OF THE UNION AND CONFEDERATE ARMIES

OFFICIAL RECORDS OF THE UNION AND CONFEDERATE NAVIES
 IN THE WAR OF THE REBELLION

HISTORICAL TIMES ILLUSTRATED ENCYCLOPEDIA OF THE CIVIL WAR

A TRAVELLER'S GUIDE TO GREAT BRITAIN SERIES

For information about National Historical Society Publications, write:
Historical Times, Inc., 2245 Kohn Road, Box 8200, Harrisburg, Pennsylvania 17105

Architectural Treasures of Early America

NEW ENGLAND BY THE SEA

From material originally published as
The White Pine Series of Architectural Monographs
edited by
Russell F. Whitehead and Frank Chouteau Brown

Lisa C. Mullins, Editor

Roy Underhill, Consultant

A Publication of
THE NATIONAL HISTORICAL SOCIETY

Library of Congress Cataloging-in-Publication Data

New England by the sea.
    (Architectural treasures of early America; 3)
      1. Architecture, Colonial — New England. 2. Architecture —
New England. I. Mullins, Lisa C. II. Series:
Architectural treasures of early America (Harrisburg,
Pa.); 3.
NA715.E27   1987   720′.974   87-11319
ISBN 0-918678-23-4

The original photographs reproduced in this publication are from the collection of drawings and photographs in "The White Pine Monograph Series, Collected and Edited by Russell F. Whitehead, The George P. Lindsay Collection." The collection, part of the research and reference collections of The American Institute of Architects, Washington, D.C., was acquired by the Institute in 1955 from the Whitehead estate, through the cooperation of Mrs. Russell F. Whitehead, and the generosity of the Weyerhauser Timber Company, which purchased the collection for presentation to the Institute. The research and reference collections of the Institute are available for public use. A written request for such use is required so that space may be reserved and assistance made available.

CONTENTS

WHITE PINE

What's all this about white pine? These architectural monographs were originally published by the White Pine Bureau as the *White Pine Monograph Series*. Why not a *Yellow Birch Monograph Series* or a *Red Oak Monograph Series?* What's the big deal with this pine tree?

Ask the woodsmen who felled it, ask the craftsman who worked it, and ask King George III who lost it. As naturalist-historian Donald Peattie wrote, "No other tree has played so great a role in the history of the American people." White pine, he declared, "built this nation, literally and figuratively."

The woodsman will tell you of its great size and abundance. The old white pines grew to be 400 years old, six feet in diameter and as tall as a twenty-story building. Old table tops and panels of knot-free wood exceeding thirty inches wide are testimony to ancient giants. Although the trees were huge, the timber was light enough to float down river to market and mill. The pines began at the ocean's edge, growing in pure stands that seemed as unending as the fortunes to be made in felling them. It is said that a squirrel could travel from Maine to the Mississippi without leaving the tops of white pine trees.

Ask the craftsman. White pine was, and is, marvelous stuff. This is the soft pine, easily dented by a fingernail, rather than the hard yellow pine of the South. Its annual rings are evenly tempered, unlike the alternating hard and soft bands of the hard pines. Very slow growth in the old forest produced the "pumpkin pine" that would "cut with almost equal ease in any direction." The look on the face of the first immigrant English joiner to work that virgin white pine must have been beautific. The creamy white shavings flowing from his plane must have raised his spirit to song.

People from far away recognized the value of this extraordinary timber. The empty pine crates used to ship Yankee goods to Charleston, South Carolina, were eagerly purchased, broken down, and put to use by the local joiners and architectural carvers. This trade of lightweight white pine into the South occasionally confounds the antique furniture buyer, misleading cursory attempts to identify southern casepieces by feeling for the greater heft given by yellow pine secondary wood (drawer sides, bottoms and the like). By the 1790's, white pine from New England was used extensively in the South, traveling on ships with figureheads carved of white pine.

Ask the English King about white pine. It was a strategic resource for the superpowers of the days of sail. The King needed the pine to make masts for his ships, and his only other sources were the often-hostile Baltic states. His American subjects, however, were felling the forests as quickly as they could. In 1761 the Crown laid claim to all white pines larger than two feet in diameter. The King's "broad arrow" blaze on a tree reserved it for masts for the Royal Navy. The colonist who molested such a tree was threatened with forfeiture of his land grant, but by this time the officials who molested such a colonist were threatened with far worse. Fighting was already underway in the pine forests before the first shots were fired at Lexington. When war came, the Americans fought beneath the white pine flag. The patriots' homes of Falmouth, Maine will not be found in this study of *New England by the Sea*. Following some unpleasantness over ship's masts, the town was flattened in 1775 by the cannon of the vengeful British.

Within a century of independence, the old growth white pine of New England was gone, Pennsylvania and New York were well worked over, and the Paul Bunyan logging of the Lake states was at its peak. The mills of the Lake states produced over three billion shingles a year for twenty-four years. The sawmill output of white pine quickly exceeded that of all other species combined.

Where the timber remained, the industry followed. The cool spine of the Appalachians dipped a high line of white pine into the South, but this last white pine boom was finished by 1915. The glory days are gone with the last of the virgin timber, but the industry that grew up around three centuries of exploitation of this tree remains powerful and sophisticated. Much of the land that was laid bare by our ancestors is now covered with the mature second-growth white pine that we use today.

What can you use to replicate the beautiful work done in the old pine? Tim Edwards, head of the millwork shop for the Colonial Williamsburg Foundation, faces this problem every day. White pine is still his top choice where freedom from warping and shrinking are important. White pine is expensive, but for the most demanding interior work, he considers the guarantee of stability well worth the extra cost. The door in the Mitchell House of Nantucket described in Chapter 5 of this volume, was made from two white pine boards, one of them twenty-seven inches wide, and was still dead flat after one hundred and fifty summers. It is often too soft for fine details, or for areas that will be exposed to wear, but you can be sure that it won't crawl away a month after you work it.

But white pine isn't the only tree in the forest. Other woods will do as well — if you select the best grades. Tulip poplar is not as stable as white pine, but it is straight grained, easily worked and takes paint beautifully. For exterior work, you are far better off using cypress. The white pine of today will not stand against decay for very long. Spruce, hemlock, yellow pine and Douglas fir suffer only from an occasional excess of resin. The problem is not so much the species, but the quality of the timber. Old, slow growth makes good wood.

Don't be surprised at craftsmen's complaints today about the declining quality of material. It's an old story. Consider the following from the pages of the *Carpenter's Company of Philadelphia Rule Book of 1786:* "The stuff also used at this time is certainly from one-sixth to one-eighth more labour than that used some years ago, it being in general so much worse — and to expect work now, under all these and many other disadvantages, for the same price by the square that the workmen had then, can hardly be deemed equitable or just."

'Twas ever thus.

ROY UNDERHILL
MASTER HOUSEWRIGHT
COLONIAL WILLIAMSBURG

Port Towns of Penobscot Bay

Text by
Charles Dana Loomis

Photographs by
The Author and Dorothy Abbot Loomis
Originally published in 1922 as White Pine Monograph
Volume VIII, Number 1

CHESTNUT STREET, CAMDEN, MAINE

PORT TOWNS OF PENOBSCOT BAY

DOWN east! How many people in these United States think at once of the rustic paraphernalia of our famous drama. But east of Boston rather than "north of Boston" lies territory rich in the history of our country. East again of the Kennebec, the traveler will find places that can still show him how the country became great, provided he turn thoughtful eyes upon them.

Three names of Maine towns on Penobscot Bay will have a familiar sound to very many ears—Camden, Belfast, Castine. It was to see for ourselves what these names were attached to that we sailed up the coast from Boston, and climbed onto the little pier under the Camden hills in very good time for the last of a remarkably fine sunrise. The rugged, barrier hills behind, the little harbor below, were a delight to the eye, but the gigantic tops of serried elms climbing away to right and left along the foreshore, the peeping white gables, and jutting massive chimneys, spoke so eloquently of old days and a long past that all doubts were gone, and we could concentrate on breakfast reassured and expectant.

After the fashion of the eighteenth-century novelist, we will leave the travelers to their refreshment and rest, and moralize at our leisure. Here is the place to make it clear that what we hoped to find were old pine-built houses worthy of record in the *White Pine Series*, and to picture what we found as monuments to a fine past and lessons for a worthy future, if you please. Looking over the whole collection of pictures, and condensing all our impressions, a general character of houses seemed so apparent that we have sought the why and wherefore, and want to try to picture this character as it was borne out by the stories of our towns, and the lives of the people who built our houses, and the kind of world they lived in.

Names have a very effective way of cutting through the layers of time to the little kernel of event that matters, and here are three names that hint at stories: Camden; there is a Camdentown in London today. Belfast; Irish linen, shipyards, and Orangemen. Castine; Mediterranean, Latin, French, certainly not Anglo-Saxon; and there we have stories well begun.

Penobscot Bay was early known as a splendid waterway, marvelously timbered and desirable, which lay so midway between French Acadia and English Virginia that no man could safely say that King James or King Louis was lord of the realm. Its waters were explored first in 1605. France established a trading post in 1629, at Bagaduce, which later became Castine. This they counted as their western outpost, and claimed all to the east of the bay as French. Later they found the Penobscot River was the great winter highway from Quebec to the Atlantic, so that the English coveted Castine, at the mouth of the river, and at last closed this door to France.

The Council of Plymouth received title to all the western shores of the bay from James I, and from this original grant, through inheritance and deed, title passed to a group of heirs. These gentlemen had great difficulties with one David Dunbar, "Surveyor of the king's woods," who requisitioned the entire coast for trees to make masts for the English navy, and forcibly stopped all colonization. The upshot of the matter was that Waldo went to London for the grantees and the Waldo Patent was confirmed in 1731. It was in 1769 that the first settler was given possession here at Camden by the "Twenty Associates," as the company of heirs was called. The town had already been named after Lord Camden, Waldo's "friend at court" during the action for the grant. The place was a hamlet when the Revolution came, and the settlers must have been terribly isolated. Small British privateers, known as Shaving Mills, swept the coast and raided Camden, sometimes with success but often the honors did not go to the king's men.

At this time Belfast also had been settled, not like Camden, by individuals sent out by a company, but by a group of people whose fathers

with his Indian allies, and is said to have married among them. As governor or commandant of what must have been a mere trading post and fort, he at least left his name for the place, which was later abandoned by the French, and finally resettled by the English in 1761. The French name does not appear to have been used until after the Revolution. The fate of the Bagaduce expedition by the Americans against this British fort may have led the townspeople to seek a name of better omen when their liberty had been won.

All this is to paint our picture of coast vil-

CARLETON HOUSE, CAMDEN, MAINE

fifty years before, in 1718, had fled from North Ireland to Boston, settled Londonderry, New Hampshire, and started the Irish potato in New England with poetic justice to become one of Maine's chief industries. A man, by name John Mitchell, came to the Belfast district, saw, and returned, to bring thirty-five of his friends, who promptly bought the site and petitioned for their ancestral name to be given it.

Castine, which now bears the name of a Count de Castine, a family since wiped out in France by the Revolution, was for a long time known as Bagaduce. The gentleman whose name it now bears was evidently an adventurous and enterprising soldier of fortune. He was a power

lages, kept from growing to towns first by the unpleasant relations of French and English and then by our own war for independence. So it was that most of our houses had to wait for their builders until the Revolution had been fought, and we can see what sort of towns the Yankees could, by sheer grit, bring into being during our lean and hungry "critical period" from 1790 to 1812. For these houses must have echoed to the rumors and alarms of the War of 1812.

Compared to most of the material that the *White Pine Series* has published, these buildings are definitely simple and austere. The character of the times is written broadly across their almost gaunt faces. But, nevertheless, there is a

Detail of Doorway   CARLETON HOUSE, CAMDEN, MAINE   *Detail of Main Façade*

MISS SMART'S COTTAGE, CHESTNUT STREET

METCALF COTTAGE, ELM STREET

COTTAGE ON MOUNTAIN STREET

THREE DOORWAYS IN CAMDEN, MAINE

real charm and an admirable character to such gauntness, especially when it is a characteristic developed on a face where inheritance and breeding are fine. That these builders were men of Massachusetts, with the background of Salem, Newburyport, Boston, Plymouth, and the settled stateliness of the Old Colony, there can be no doubt. It is interesting to see what they retained of their birthright, and what their modest means obliged them to forego.

of the American sailing ships, and was the home of a fleet of merchant sailors who made every port from Liverpool to Bankok. *Castine* was painted under the stern of many a windjammer known in the Indies and the China Seas.

Though our houses must have been nearly coeval, they divide into three general types: the one-story cottage, the two-story gabled farm-house, and the square, hipped-roof mansion, with interior chimneys.

HOUSE ON CHESTNUT STREET, CAMDEN, MAINE

In Camden the simpler types prevail and there is little rich detail. In Belfast a large number of Neo-Grec or Classic Revival houses complicate the situation. They give the town an air almost of opulence, and date its heyday thirty years later than Camden, in the time when whaling and lumber were beginning to make men's fortunes. All this work we have purposely omitted and stuck to the houses of earlier date. In Castine, both the fullness of detail and its very colonial character point both to an earlier date and a less limited financial condition. This town was the best known of the three during the days

In Camden we have the three types all well represented. Of the cottage types only the doorways have been chosen for reproduction, but the pictures on page 16 give one a fair idea of the height of the façade, the ample wall, and widely spaced windows. The very considerable height from window head to cornice should be noted. This logical result of a good half-story under the roof is often slighted in our modern adaptations, to the detriment of the façade. All these cottages were originally built with a large central chimney, and a minute stairway, built between chimney and front door, in a tiny entrance hall.

SMALL HOUSE, BELFAST, MAINE

STEVENS HOUSE, BELFAST, MAINE

Of the gabled farmhouses, two in Camden, one shown on page 12 and one on page 17, and a fine example in Belfast, on page 18, with arched entrance doors both on the street and in the gable end, illustrate this more commodious type of dwelling enlarged from the cottage. They still have considerable length of plan and the great central chimney.

The more well-to-do citizens, however, seem to have universally seized on the square plan, with two chimneys built into the cross wall dividing the front from the back rooms. The great

thrice removed influence of the illustrious Adam brothers. The universally over-delicate mouldings, the lack of projection of the cornices, the very delicate sash and window frames, the almost universal frontispiece door, in preference to a porch, point not so much to poverty as to the following of a model. The model is not hard to find in Massachusetts, where the Adam influence came by way of the handbooks from England. These books are well known, and were the usual guides of the carpenter designers. The restraint of this work in Maine cannot be en-

BENJAMIN FIELD HOUSE, BELFAST, MAINE

depth of plan resulting from such a scheme necessitated the hip roof, and the pitch seems to have been flattened through economy even lower than the Massachusetts prototype. In every case the fenestration is excellent, the openings broad and ample, and the wall spaces kept even wider than the windows, commonly by grouping the side windows in pairs and thus gaining exterior wall surface even when the shutters were open. With no exceptions the windows were kept well away from the corners, and all the houses show a fine wide corner pier and have a resulting air of solidity.

With the possible exception of those in Castine, these houses all show decidedly the

tirely ascribed to poverty, for the mouldings are good in profile, the doorways well designed, and the finish never stinted. It would have cost no more to coarsen all the detail, or to misplace the motives of the composition. They succeeded in achieving a grand manner in the most straightforward way. They stuck to good proportion, they used forms throughout which had been demonstrated successful for execution in wood, and they erred on the side of simplicity and thinness of details, both admirable faults in buildings built of wood. Clapboards were kept uniformly very narrow, and even the side and cross rails of the shutters were made narrow on the face, to keep in scale with the other detail:

Detail of Side Porch

JOHNSON HOUSE, CASTINE, MAINE

Detail of Corner

no attempt was made to use stone derived quoins, cornices, or pilasters, and the frontispiece doorways were so refined and attenuated as to lose their stone-cut character. These are as frankly wood-built houses as could be asked for.

A few of the details are worth notice. The frontispiece doorways nearly all have the overhead fanlight in form of an arch either round or elliptical, sometimes glazed, sometimes filled with a wooden slab fan. Is it not possible that

photograph of the Johnson House in Castine, page 21, are frequent and deserve respectful study for their wooden scale and richness combined with simplicity. Notice, too, in this picture the thoroughly workmanlike and pleasing way in which the brick end has been joined with the clapboarded front. It becomes frankly a brick end due to two enormous end chimneys, and not a brick house finished with wood, as sometimes appears when the thickness of the brick wall shows on the front. The little side

PERKINS HOUSE — 1769 — CASTINE MAINE

the absence of porches is partly due to the extremely mild summers, and the dark winters, requiring maximum light in the stair hall entry? It is noticeable that the doors are frequently fitted with slat shutters, which again shows the desire for a modified ventilation in the breezy summer afternoons. It is a pity that so many of the present owners have painted their sash black or dark green. The loss of the sparkle of the brilliant muntins in the dark openings is a serious one. Screens and screen doors are accursed by photographers of architecture. Some one can make a fortune by the invention of an invisible screen door, but not too invisible.

Cornices of the general type shown in the

porch of this house is mainly wood — no attempt here to ape stone forms. The cap is gotten out of one stick with the shaft, and the diminution and entasis result. The stable wing of the Adams House at Castine, shown on page 23, is certainly playful enough use of stone forms. This is not a functional arcade, but it is good carpentry, and pretty good composition too.

Lack of space forbids the reproduction of the little church on the green at Castine. It is a smaller scale variant of the Belfast church, and the latter was probably built afterward, and is doubtless an echo. It is certainly more successful as far as the tower goes, and shows improvements in detail but lacks the charm of the little

Doorway
PERKINS HOUSE, CASTINE, MAINE

other doorways this seems to be much more obviously of stone origin. Its wide, flat faces and broad, well-curved mouldings and thick fillets are much more early Georgian than what we usually call Colonial. Perhaps the model came rather from Sir William Chambers than Robert Adam. Notice, too, the excessive entasis of the pilasters.

That no one ever reads an architectural article to the bitter end is a commonplace among architects, so perhaps we are safe in stepping out before the falling curtain and speaking an epilogue to the empty house. Let us be as old-fashioned as our houses, and point a moral.

In these days, when financial solons cry to the world, "Work and save," and the man in the street sees dollars grow as big as harvest moons, the simple house of wood is suddenly a thing of virtue, preaching economy by the roadside. These Penobscot houses, simple to baldness, built in similar stringent times, embody all the virtues we would like to practise: rigid economy, dignity, good taste, good proportion, refinement, honesty, and, in spite of austerity, charm. If any of our pictures or any of our words help toward these results in the plain houses of to-day, this article has not been amiss.

one-story structure, which, without galleries, can have a fine side-window motive.

The Perkins House at Castine must be placed in a paragraph by itself. It stands alone among our collection as a pre-Revolutionary example. The mass and the character are frankly English, foursquare, and solid. It is evident that the ell toward the road is an addition, in fact that patching of the clapboarding is visible in the photograph. Neither Asher Benjamin nor Batty Langley had anything to do with this house. The steep pitch of the roof, the heavy solid frames of the windows, moulded and doweled, projecting far outside the clapboards, the unevenly divided sash with twenty lights, the blunt cornice, nowhere show the Adam influence. In fact the date of the original house is 1769, and the addition can have been but little later. The vestibule porch is comparatively modern, but is well handled and adds materially to the general effect of the house.

The detail photograph of the doorway gives one also a fair idea of the window frames and sash, and the unusual location of the glass practically on the same plane as the clapboards. This detail also occurs in the oldest house in Camden, otherwise ruinously altered. It may be a stretch of the imagination, but in contrast to all our

Stable Wing
ADAMS HOUSE, CASTINE, MAINE

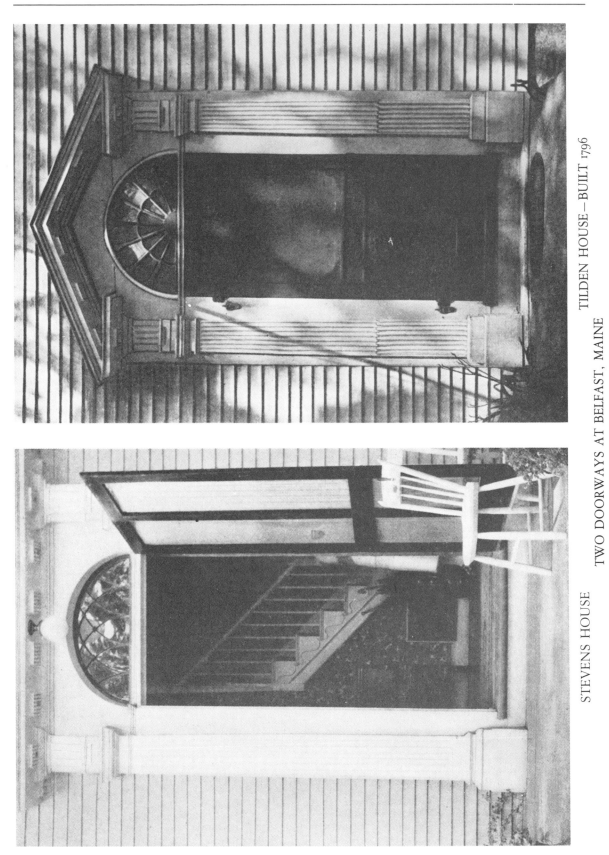

TILDEN HOUSE—BUILT 1796

STEVENS HOUSE

TWO DOORWAYS AT BELFAST, MAINE

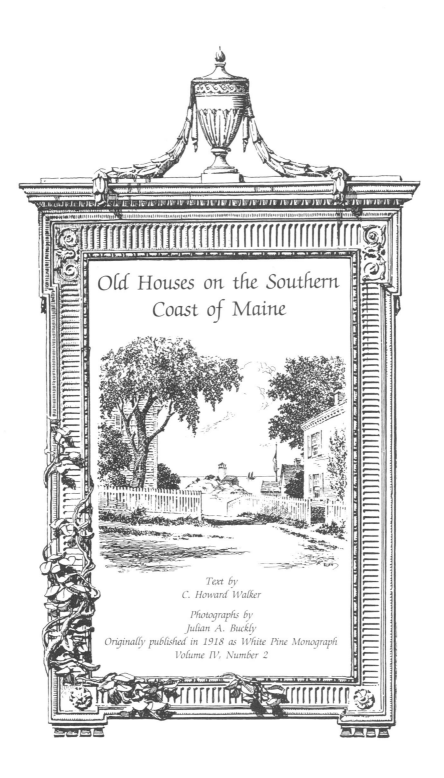

Old Houses on the Southern
Coast of Maine

Text by
C. Howard Walker

Photographs by
Julian A. Buckly

Originally published in 1918 as White Pine Monograph
Volume IV, Number 2

JEWETT HOUSE, SOUTH BERWICK, MAINE

A remarkably well proportioned and delicate Roman Doric porch. Note the filling of the
flutes in the lower third of the columns to avoid too great apparent slenderness in the columns.

SOME OLD HOUSES ON THE SOUTHERN COAST OF MAINE

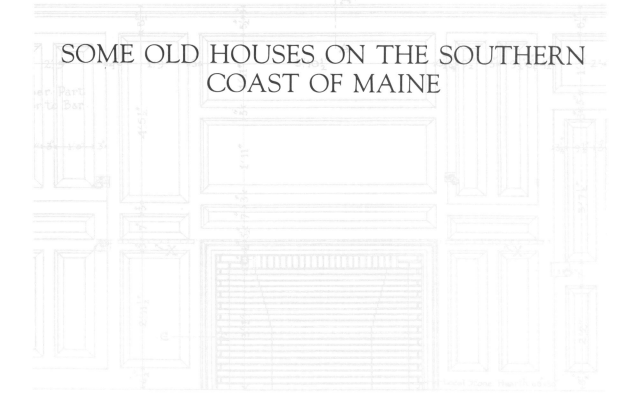

THE Yankee skipper feeling his way in the soft fog that lies along the southern Maine coast in August, watching the chart spread in the wheelhouse beside him, sees upon it the lines of the streams flowing southerly into the sea, as the rain drops run down a windowpane at the beginning of a shower. They waver in their courses as they swerve around highlands, now reaching straight through meadows and spreading into inland ponds, now tortuously winding amidst rocky ledges, but always tending southeasterly until they form estuaries up which the sea tide rushes to meet the waters from the forests and the hills.

Down these streams float the rafts of lumber from the pinelands, cut in the forests of Aroostook, and at the headwaters of the Androscoggin, the Penobscot, and the Kennebec. Deep in the forests, far up on the mountain side, lie the camps, busy through the white winters with the work of many lumbermen who are felling the monarchs of the trees, the tall, slender, straight white pines of the northland.

It is a strange anomaly that the white pine, with its home in a land of harsh winters, growing amidst the constant stress of wind and storm, should have a fiber straight as a ruled line, a surface soft and smooth as silk, and that its grain, instead of being gnarled and twisted, should be so even and fine that it will respond to the most delicate of carving.

The logs, brought down over the snows to the streams, float down in broad rafts to the more open reaches of the rivers, to the mill ponds where the streams are dammed, and there are sawn in lengths and widths, into scantling and plank and board, and sent to their destinations.

The Yankee skipper knows all of this. He has loaded his decks at the head of navigation and is now distributing his cargo. He knows every inch of the varied coast of Maine, the long fingers of land stretching out into the sea, the inlets, and bays, and islands, and reefs; and even in the fog he has little need of his chart, but the chart itself shows penetrating arms of the sea running deep into the land to meet the rivers, each of which ramifies into little bays and coves and back waters and into numerous almost land-locked harbors in which navies might ride. And, like the Greeks of Leigh Hunt, the skipper "is always putting up harbors and creeks," for there lie his markets which he can supply from the source directly.

The coast cities of Maine lie up these inlets, and in the cities and upon the banks of the bays and coves the merchants of Maine built their houses.

The first century after the Revolutionary War was one of active shipping interest in New England. The East India trade created a long and famous list of clipper ships, which gave prosperity not only to Salem, Newburyport and Portsmouth, but to Portland and Bath and other Maine coast towns.

The whaling fleets of Martha's Vineyard, Nantucket and New Bedford were aided by the Maine shipyards, and both commerce and shipbuilding industry brought prosperity.

In the years between the end of the Revolu-

manded them and sailed from and came home to their own doors.

There are no more numerous or better land-locked harbors for "fitting out," while safely protected from all interference, than on the coast of Maine. The Dalmatian coast of the Adriatic and the gulfs of the Grecian peninsula alone compare with it. The famous *Bonhomme Richard* of John Paul Jones was fitted out in the Great Bay up the Piscataqua River, and many a cargo has been laden from some concealed nook between York and Campobello.

HOBBS HOUSE, SOUTH BERWICK, MAINE
A very simple house of unusually good proportions.

tionary War and the War of 1812 there is increasing evidence of comfortable fortunes having been amassed by local merchants all along the Atlantic coast, for larger and more important private houses are being built everywhere, not only in the towns themselves, but often at quite a distance from them. Especially is this the case in the first decade of the nineteenth century.

Sheltered from the sea by outlying islands, as at North Haven, or nestled in behind promontories or headlands, with still waters at the foot of grassy slopes, are to be found the homes of these amphibiously minded merchants of Maine, men who sent out their own ships and often com-

Our Yankee skipper has been standing in closer to land, and suddenly he runs out of the fog into clear sunshine. As he emerges the long white mass of mist stretches right and left like a sheer wall but by a knife. It seems as if by looking back he might see in it the hole he had left in emerging. The land breeze, dry and hot, is beating the fog out to sea, and before him is spread the charming fantastic coast of Maine: rocky ledges, gray at their crowns and russet and red and purple as they dip into the tide, upon their tops and sides twisted cedars and hardy savins, long reaches of green salt marsh, deeper touches of upland meadow, and every-

SEWELL HOUSE, YORK, MAINE

Finely proportioned façade, simple fence with delicate urns, the square balusters to the fence are set diagonally to obtain the play of light and shade.

HOUSE AT WELLS, MAINE
Well-proportioned façade, with wall texture refined by narrow clapboards.

JUDGE HAYES HOUSE, SOUTH BERWICK, MAINE
Gabled type, ample in effect. Balustrade over porch unnecessary, too high.

where little or large inlets setting into the land.

Over the crest of one of these rocky hillocks are broad masses of spreading elms, grouped together as if planted with a purpose. That purpose is manifest as the point of land is weathered and the inlet opens, for amidst the trees is a broad white mass, a simple rectangular shape, set four-square to the winds, with a low-pitched roof and ample chimneys above it at each end. It is nestled among the trees, which were planted

apparent importance of the house with which they are associated. But there may be a long L of outbuildings, or a considerable barn.

Many of the houses in Maine were built between 1800 and 1810. That decade is an important one in residential building in American Eastern cities. The early economies of the years following the Revolutionary War were no longer felt necessary, and comfortable living, such as had been in the Colonies before the great struggle, began to reappear.

ROBERT LORD HOUSE, KENNEBUNK, MAINE
Type simulating stone upon façade by the use of matched sidings.

to give it shade from the summer's sun, and is the homestead of some merchant of Maine, or at least was such in the early days of the last century, and may at the present time be the summer home of a resident from a distant city.

It corresponds in a way with the planters' homes of Virginia, though it has no dependencies of the slave quarters, nor buildings for the housing of farm laborers. For the farm laborer of the North has usually a little home of his own at a distance. Also the income of this homestead is not necessarily from the farm; it comes from merchant shipping, so that very often the farm buildings seem disproportionately small for the

The traditions of Colonial architecture had not been disturbed by the turgid stream from other sources that later appeared. When relations were reestablished with England, importations of the minor factors of house building again made their appearance. Hardware, wallpapers, relief ornaments for mantels, etc., were often brought from London, but a skilled race of New England carpenters and of carvers had been created who, however, manifestly looked to the English pattern books, published and republished since 1700, for their designs of mouldings, cornices, and entablatures, for portals, and even for façades, which latter fact somewhat accounts

ROBERT LORD HOUSE, KENNEBUNK, MAINE

Details especially good. Balustrade at top too weak at the corner. Sentinel window
in gable upon entrance axis is out of harmony with the shape of the other openings.

SMITH HOUSE, WISCASSET, MAINE

Admirable cornices, both upon main façade and the smaller masses. Note
the angle of these cornices is more acute than 45 degrees, which is usually
the case in Colonial exteriors, and gives an effect of additional refinement.

for the custom of often confining the architectural treatment to the façade alone, leaving the other elevations largely to take care of themselves, and also for the different surface treatment of façades to imitate stone antecedents, while the ends were frankly clapboarded or at times built of brick.

The classic styles originated in wood, the columns were tree trunks, the facias boards, the mouldings cleats; and the reversion to wood in America was the most natural thing in the world.

cess of material, their charm being that of simplicity without crudeness, based upon proportions obtained from the books of English masters.

The work in New England, somewhat more indigenous than elsewhere in the States, was more refined in its detail than elsewhere. There is more attention paid to entasis of columns, to fineness of fillets, to subtlety of curved profiles to mouldings. The fact is interesting, for English detail was less careful in contrasting sections, and in delicacy and avoidance of monot-

SMITH HOUSE, WISCASSET, MAINE
Extremely well proportioned, having almost monumental
quality. There is a good portal behind the storm porch.

The style was going back to its original ancestry and in doing so became delicate and refined. For there is nothing so manifestly absurd as an excessive use of bulk of wood, both for aesthetic and structural reasons. The classic wooden architecture of New England gives evidence of a very intelligent use of the material, which was maintained after the Georgian style in England became heavy and dull and cumbrous. That this is largely due to an appreciation of the possibilities of wood, and of white pine especially, is constantly manifest. Seldom in these houses of the early nineteenth century is there ex-

ony. A comparison of Virginian Colonial details which were derived at a better period directly from England justifies this statement.

It is known that many of the New England carpenters were also ship carpenters and figurehead carvers, and there is no education relating to the beauty of lines and curves better than that obtained in designing ships. An appreciation of line and form became second nature to these men, and when it was associated with so admirable and amenable a material as white pine, it would be strange indeed if the results were not good.

Detail of Entrance
SEWELL HOUSE, YORK, MAINE
Dignified portal with adequate arch moulding. Note
that the pilasters as well as the columns have entases.

Necessary economies also created the restraint so essential in fine classic architecture. An interesting example of this is shown by the illustrations of two houses in Wiscasset. One, the William Nickels House, was built in 1807–1808, and has both upon piazza and the house itself a very admirable Corinthian order without modillions but with double rows of contrasting dentils, Greek in feeling. The piazza balustrade was unfortunately added about 1890 with no regard for or knowledge of the charm of the old work. Mr. Abiel Wood began his house in 1812 with

distinction. Classic architecture originates as a one-storied style, it progresses as a two-storied style, and later still more stories are added. The difficulty of adding these stories successfully increases geometrically with the increasing number of stories. This must necessarily be the case, as with the addition of each story the design departs farther from the original source of its inspiration. Therefore some of the smaller and simpler two-storied houses of more modest type built outside the towns are sometimes the more attractive.

ABIEL WOOD HOUSE, WISCASSET, MAINE
Simple and well proportioned.

the distinct intention of outdoing the Nickels House, but had to practice economy, and, taking several years to complete the house, omitted the pilaster treatment; yet the house is bettered in its proportions, especially in those of the Palladian windows in the second story, and the arched window over it in the third story. This latter window is a favorite terminal factor of the axis motive of a façade in houses on the Maine coast, though not peculiar to them.

The question of proportions is always somewhat intangible and often houses with the least embellishment give an impression of the greater

It was to such houses as these that the coaster brought her lumber, landing it on the shore below the site, where the frame was cut and mortised and tenoned and pinned, with the strong corner posts which so often show in the rooms and become cased pilasters. It was here that, after each side had been put together upon the ground, the day of the house-raising was observed, bringing together the interested neighbors and celebrated by a liberal distribution of hard cider to the workmen. And later the coasters bring the boards and sidings and clapboards, and the stock of greater thickness for the pilasters, all of which is planed and fitted to as near perfection as the carpenter, proud of his reputation for skill, can perform his work. The fluted columns, the dentil courses with the infinite variations, which characterize so much of this work, were probably done in a neighboring town, of the finest, clearest white pine, without a blemish, thoroughly dried, and a pleasure to look upon even before it was touched by a plane. The carving may have come from farther afield. Pieces of English carving in mahogany made by some London master, even perhaps by Grinling Gibbons himself, have been found behind the paint of New England mantels, having been imported and used as models and repeated in the remainder of the work in white pine.

Two of the simpler two-storied buildings are illustrated: one the Hobbs House at South Berwick, the other at Wells, not many miles away; one on the river, the other not far from the shore. The Hobbs House could not be simpler, but its proportions are admirable, and the details refined. Its hopper roof is surmounted by a balustrade of plain cylindrical balusters, well spaced.

In studying the books from which the carpenters worked, it will be noticed that they are lacking in examples of good turnings, and the weakest details of many otherwise excellent Colonial designs are in the balusters. This is not the case with staircase balusters. The Hobbs House balustrade and the fence to the Sewell House at York, indicate that turnings are not necessary, and that they may be too small in scale for the rest of the work.

The smaller houses seldom are covered with the broad matched sidings which were used to give the appearance of the smooth surface of a stone ashlar face. This work was confined to the more ambitious examples and upon their main façades. But the clapboards which covered most of the walls were not of the coarse modern variety, laid as per specification 4¼ inches to the weather. On the contrary, they were clear and thin and often laid three inches to the weather, and at times the widths of the overlaps were graded up the wall. The fine narrow spaces between the shadow lines gave scale and texture to the wall surface. These narrow clapboards are to be seen upon the Wells and York houses.

The Smith House at Wiscasset has a broad overlapping siding. This house is unusually fine in its proportions. Its end walls are brick, the thickness of the wall, painted white, showing at the ends of the façade. The cornices are fine in their thin overshooting angle, but the Ionic cap is heavy in its scrolls. The balustrade is very well proportioned to the mass of the house. The Sewell House at York has great distinction in proportions and an unusually fine portal with Ionic columns in antis. The broad simplicity of the details of the house and its vigor of treatment are exceptional. It has the dignity of late Georgian work with the finesse of the Colonial.

In the towns themselves, as in Salem and Newburyport and Portsmouth, the old sea captains and merchants built their houses almost directly upon the streets, the gardens at the back. These houses are treated usually with pilasters, either Ionic or Corinthian, running through two stories. If the house has three stories the lower story is made, as in the old Dole House in Portland and the Nickels House at Wiscasset, a high base or podium for the upper stories, not, as often occurs elsewhere, with the pilaster in the first two stories, and the third story an attic above the entablature. The outer pilasters are kept well in from the corner, thus announcing the fact that the architectural treatment is for ornament only. Also the entablature breaks thoroughly, the break being carried through the cyma, not stopping at the soffit of the facia, or planceer. The definition of stories by a belt course is usual, but not universal.

On the old Dole House the very delicate porch is surmounted by a villainous balustrade.

It will be noted in several of these houses that the center axis is accented by a third-story arched window, between the square openings at the sides. This is one of Palladio's novelties, of which he had several. It always looks interpolated, and is at its worst when the arch is doubled concentrically as in the Nickels House. It is a favorite motive in the first decade of the nineteenth century and an ill-advised one. A glance at the Sewell House at York will show that its omission is a virtue.

In the illustrations of portals, that of the Jewett House at South Berwick is unusually fine, and the treatment of fine herringbone reeds in the pilasters of the Nickels House is unique and shows how effective can be a very simple method of obtaining interesting texture.

And so our skipper sails up the river, anchors off a pier, goes ashore in his boat, and spends his afternoon in the counting-house of one of the ship-owners, who is also a builder of the dignified houses of Maine. He may have done so in the early part of the last century, he may do so today, for still are the forests being felled, still is the white pine being sawn and planed and chiseled and carved, still are the houses being built, and, by good fortune, following the good old styles of years ago.

Detail of Entrance Doorway
NICKELS HOUSE, WISCASSET, MAINE

Interesting textures obtained by very simple means. The graduation of the reeds and darts in the arch from the same center as the divisions of the fanlight, instead of being at right angles to the arch curve, is unusual, as is also the herringbone reeding of the pilasters.

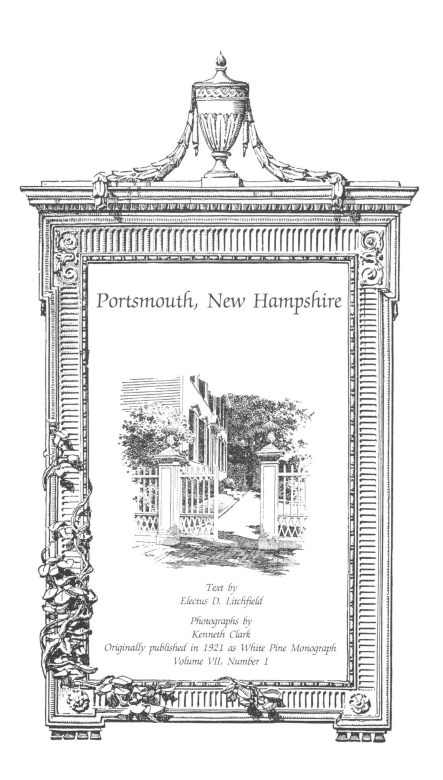

Portsmouth, New Hampshire

Text by
Electus D. Litchfield

Photographs by
Kenneth Clark
Originally published in 1921 as White Pine Monograph
Volume VII, Number 1

TREADWELL HOUSE — 1750 — PORTSMOUTH, NEW HAMPSHIRE

PORTSMOUTH, NEW HAMPSHIRE:
AN EARLY AMERICAN METROPOLIS

ANNO Domini 1630 saw the beginnings of Portsmouth. Twenty years after the first permanent settlement at Jamestown, and but ten years after the landing of the Pilgrims at Plymouth Rock, John Mason and his associates sailed into Portsmouth Harbor and established upon its shore the first settlement of the New Hampshire colony. No mere chance determined the site. The wooded and gently sloping shore of this beautiful and convenient harbor affording a safe haven for sailing craft on a "storm and rock-bound coast," was a logical selection. From a collection of a few small huts, the town grew and increased in importance for two hundred years. Time was when Portsmouth bid fair to be a commercial rival of New York, and in the early centuries of American history its part is written large upon the record. It reached the zenith of its development in the first years of the nineteenth century, but the invention of the steamboat and the coming of the iron-hulled deep-draft vessel marked the beginning of the end of Portsmouth's commercial supremacy. While from that time Portsmouth does not seem to have gone noticeably forward, perhaps because of the beauty of its location and the healthfulness of its climate, or because the Government continued to maintain there an important naval station, it nevertheless does not seem to have gone backward. It is today no decayed nor deserted city, but one which has seemed to hold miraculously unchanged the quiet and romantic character that it possessed as the home of many of the best and most distinguished citizens of our late Colonial and early Republican periods.

To the architect and the historian the city of Portsmouth makes a special appeal. Other towns have retained much of their early flavor, but in none of them, as in Portsmouth, do we have a whole community the character of which has not really changed for a century. The summer tourist may think of Portsmouth only as a railway center from which he passes to Rye Beach or the Isles of Shoals, and remember alone the orange cake for which one of its modest confectioneries is noted; but to one whose eyes are open and whose mind is attuned to the memories with which its streets and docks and homes are filled, this old town has an eduring charm. For this ancient metropolis played a stirring part in our early history. It was here the expedition started which captured Louisburg, and high in the steeple of old St. John's Church still hangs the bell that pealed over that early capital of New France. Paul Revere was no stranger to the New Hampshire town, and an earlier ride of his, not chronicled in verse, provided powder and shot used at Lexington and Bunker Hill. Here lived Governor Langdon, that stalwart patriot who pledged all his money and a warehouse of Jamaica rum to provide uniforms and arms for Stark's Continentals, who at Bennington won lasting fame and saved Mollie Stark from widowhood. The docks of Portsmouth were no less familiar to John Paul Jones than the quarter-deck of the *Bonhomme Richard,* and on foggy nights his spirit and those of a galaxy of other gallant heroes still wend their way through its well-loved streets to the Yard. When the moon is just right you can see them: Hull of the *Constitution*, Decatur, Bainbridge, and the gallant Lawrence, and after they have passed, great men of a later day,—Franklin Pierce and Daniel

Webster, and a host of others. There are memories here, too, of statesmen of our own generation who met and signed the treaty which ended the Russo-Japanese War. Portsmouth has played no mean part in history, but, after all, it is not that which holds for us its greatest interest. It is because it stands today, just as it stood more than a hundred years ago, simple and unostentatious, and yet clearly the home which must have been very gentle and very fine. They are still full of exquisite furniture and china which are the envy of collectors; portraits by Copley and other distinguished painters abound, and help us in imagination to see those gentlewomen of that early day with powdered hair and flowing silks, colonial governors and other imposing dignitaries in velvets, young blades in knee-breeches and satin waistcoats,

GOVERNOR LANGDON HOUSE—1784—PORTSMOUTH, NEW HAMPSHIRE

of an early American "Four Hundred." There is an atmosphere of elegance and refinement in the old city of Portsmouth not found often in America. The wealth of many other colonial towns is physically more evident. Portsmouth has no street of wealthy "nabobs" like Chestnut Street in Salem; and even to such a discerning eye as that of George Washington, when he visited Portsmouth after his inauguration, the pine-built homes of Portsmouth seemed "inconsiderable," compared to the brick mansions of Virginia. But these houses stand today a unique record of a civilization and a culture dining tables groaning under their weight of damask and silver, fine wines in glittering decanters, and the rarest of china from the Orient.

It is a snug and well built city. Twice or three times fire had swept across it, and, rebuilt, it seems to have been each time better than before. Not a city of great mansions with outbuildings for slaves and other retainers, but a city of homes of high-bred, God-fearing gentlemen; for if architecture can record, as it surely does, the character of a people, it writes large in Portsmouth the refinement and gentility of that early town.

The author regrets that a later volume (Vol-

GOVERNOR BENNING WENTWORTH HOUSE—1750—LITTLE HARBOR, PORTSMOUTH, NEW HAMPSHIRE

BUCKMINSTER HOUSE, PORTSMOUTH, NEW HAMPSHIRE

Built in 1720 by Daniel Warner.

distinguished examples of this unusual type.

It is characteristic of Portsmouth that its houses are essentially city houses, and not, as in so many other places, suburban dwellings swallowed up by the city. It is characteristic, too, of Portsmouth that, with but three important exceptions, its houses are uniformly of wood.

We are apt to remember of most of our New England towns, a few houses of special architectural merit which stand out against a background of others of the simplest character; but in Portsmouth the standard of all the houses is so high that it is a virtue that our illustrations are taken from the rank and file of its early buildings rather than those of special outstanding merit. Some of the most charming of them are of the Wendell House, built by Jeremiah Hill in 1789 at the corner of Edward and Pleasant streets. Its exterior

ume IX, Chapter 7) tells of the "Three-Story Colonial House in New England," and thus took from this paper the pictures of several of Portsmouth's most important houses. Nowhere as here was the three-story American house of wood so successfully and consistently developed. The Haven House, built about 1800, with its well designed fence, after the manner of McIntire in Salem; the Governor Woodbury Mansion, built in 1809 by Samuel Ham; the Langley Boardman House, with its charming Palladian window and delightful semicircular porch, its unique mahogany door paneled with oval inserts or mouldings in whalebone; the Ladd, or Moffit, House, with its magnificent interiors; and last, but not least, the John Pierce House on Court Street, with its well designed façade, its delightful stairway, and interesting plan, are all

HOUSE AT 363 STATE STREET,
PORTSMOUTH, NEW HAMPSHIRE

JACOB WENDELL HOUSE, PORTSMOUTH, NEW HAMPSHIRE
Built in 1789 by Jeremiah Hill.

Entrance Detail
JACOB WENDELL HOUSE—1789—PORTSMOUTH, NEW HAMPSHIRE

Entrance Detail
HOUSE AT 271 COURT STREET, PORTSMOUTH, NEW HAMPSHIRE

is of clapboards set a few inches to the weather, like so many other houses of northern New England. It is delightful in mass as well as in detail. The door, of twelve panels, beautifully designed, carries, it would seem, the original knocker and an ancient door-plate, while in the broken pediment above is set a most interesting feature consisting of a whale-oil lamp carved in wood, set upon an ornamental base, suggesting the source of the wealth of its original owner. A close examination of the detailed photograph will

It would have been so easy to have made the railing of the usual and accepted height, and to have missed the scale which it lends to the whole composition.

The little house at 314 Court Street is of piquant interest. The frame of the entrance door is delightfully original and interesting, but it is terribly marred in its effect by the modern door and transom within it. How many architects have passed this house and wished that they might have the courage to ring the bell and

HOUSE AT 124 PLEASANT STREET, PORTSMOUTH, NEW HAMPSHIRE

discover a repetition of the lamp motif in the pediments of the dormers. It is interesting to find this record of the owner embodied in the architecture of his house, and a pity it is, that one so seldom finds such a personal note. It is a pleasing indication of the early interest of architect and owner in the details of its construction; but wherever one turns in a careful study of this modest and unassuming structure there is found the evidence of the affectionate interest of its designer. Notice such seemingly unimportant things as the mouldings at the chimney-caps, the sweep and proportion of the granite steps and copings, the height and the detail of the iron posts and rails.

ask its history, or to suggest the pleasure that it would give them to set inside that charming frame a door and fanlight which would be in keeping!

The houses at 124 Pleasant Street; Livermore Street; and the Samuel Lord House are quite of the general run of Portsmouth's houses. They are simple, straightforward buildings, two windows flanking on each side an interesting doorway in the first story, and with five windows across the front in the second, the roof being hipped or gambreled, as the case may be, and, in the case of the Lord House now occupied by the Portsmouth Historical Society, pierced with dormers. This house, historically as well as architecturally, is the most important of the three, as it was the home of John Paul Jones during his residence in Portsmouth.

The fence and fenceposts for all these houses are well designed, and recall those built in Salem during the same period. Those who planned them had no hesitancy in combining carefully cut granite bases and steps with wood fences and posts. It is of value to note that though built more than a hundred years ago, the work in the close-spaced clapboards, the studied disposition of windows and doors, together with the charming detail of its window heads, entrance door, and trim. It should be an incentive to the architectural draftsman of today to realize how much genuine pleasure there is in the contemplation of this studied, but simple, building. It is the sort of thing "anybody could do," yet almost nobody can. It has the qualities of great monumental architecture—correct proportion, simplicity, and interest.

SAMUEL LORD HOUSE, PORTSMOUTH, NEW HAMPSHIRE
Built in 1730 by Captain Purcell. The home of John Paul Jones during his stay in Portsmouth.

wood shows no greater signs of decay than the New Hampshire granite itself. The house at 363 State Street has a latter-day American basement effect, with its steps and entrance door recessed within the front wall. The Doric columns of its addition and the slight modifications in its detail would indicate that it was made some years after the building of the original house.

There is something delightfully satisfying about the old house on Meeting House Hill, and it is valuable to analyze its charm. It seems to consist in the fine texture given by

An interesting architectural fragment is shown on page 47 of the doorway of 271 Court Street. Here is the rounded pediment found often in Portsmouth and traceable, perhaps, to French influences.

The Governor Langdon House, though not the largest, is perhaps the most pretentious of the wood houses of Portsmouth. We can believe that no money was spared in its construction, and it has suffered from the consequent over-richness of its design. Its Corinthian capitals are marvels of wood carving and of preserva-

HOUSE AT 314 COURT STREET

HOUSE ON LIVERMORE STREET

TWO DOORWAYS AT PORTSMOUTH, NEW HAMPSHIRE

tion. This was the home of the early Governor of New Hampshire who pledged his means for the Continental cause, and within its walls have been entertained admirals, generals, and world-renowned statesmen of more than one generation.

The Wentworth-Gardner House stands upon a terrace shaded by a magnificent linden, and looks out across beautiful Portsmouth Harbor.

of stone ashlar, but might well pardon its architect when he studies its delightful proportions and details, both in exterior and interior. The house as photographed is not quite as it was built. Some of its interest is due to the fascinating doorway with scrolled pediment and gilded pineapple applied by its recent owner. There are not many towns where there is anything much finer than the interior of this house,

WENTWORTH-GARDNER HOUSE — 1760 — PORTSMOUTH, NEW HAMPSHIRE

It is with mixed feelings one learns that it has been bought by the Metropolitan Museum, and that perhaps even by this time its interiors have been transplanted to New York. Its location is quite apart from the other best residences of Portsmouth, and in a section of the town which perhaps most shows its age. One cannot help regretting that the house could not have been maintained, perhaps by the city of Portsmouth, or perhaps by the state of New Hampshire. A purist like Ruskin might criticize the design of the façade, made as it is in wood in imitation

but there are so many other towns where it seems so much harder to keep the fine old things, that one regrets that it is one of Portsmouth's houses that had to be taken.

Thus ends our little glimpse of this ancient metropolis. There is so much more to be said, and so much there to be seen, that this ending, like that of school, should be but the commencement. For the student of American architecture no sojourn will be happier or of more lasting value than the time he spends in this delightful city.

Detail of Doorway
HOUSE AT 43 MEETING HOUSE HILL, PORTSMOUTH, NEW HAMPSHIRE

Newburyport, Massachusetts

Text by
Richard Arnold Fisher

Photographs by
Julian A. Buckly

Originally published in 1917 as White Pine Monograph
Volume III, Number 3

Detail of Entrance and Front Façade
GOVERNOR WILLIAM DUMMER HOUSE, BYFIELD, MASSACHUSETTS
The doorway is almost Jacobean in character, which is a type seldom found in
this vicinity. The house is now used by the Headmaster of Dummer Academy.

OLD HOUSES IN AND AROUND
NEWBURYPORT, MASSACHUSETTS

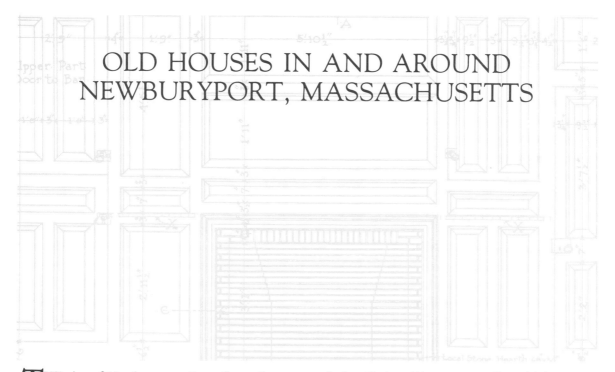

THE city of Newburyport lies a few miles up-stream from the mouth of the river Mer-rimack, which forms its harbor, and was, at one period of its early and greater days, second in importance only to Boston among New England seaports. This was in the early years of the nineteenth century, when Massachusetts ships were to be seen in most of the harbors of the world; in the year 1804 it is recorded that the duties collected in Massachusetts exceeded even those of New York. This was the time when Newburyport was at the height of its prosperity, the receipts of its Custom House ranking third among Massachusetts ports of entry, and its imports in a single month reaching the value of more than three-quarters of a million dollars. In the year 1805 its fleet numbered one hundred and seventy-three ships and other vessels of good size, exclusive of smaller craft not listed. Shipbuilding was also an important industry there, and at one period one hundred vessels were under construction at the same time. A number of frigates and sloops of war were built in its yards, and later on some of the swift clipper ships, such as the renowned *Dreadnought,* that made the American merchant marine famous.

One generally hears that Newburyport was founded in 1635, but, strictly speaking, that is the date of settlement of the town of Newbury, from which Newburyport was set off in the middle of the eighteenth century. The two towns still form one community in a geographical and social sense. The original settlement was not on the Merrimack, but on the shores of the Parker River, a smaller tidal stream lying a mile or two farther toward the south. The early settlers formed a farming community, but the proximity of the Merrimack led naturally to the upbuilding of sea trade, and long before the time of the Revolution it had become a shipping center of considerable importance. Its traffic was largely with England and the continent of Europe, while that of Salem was more with the East Indies, a difference having its origin, it is said, in the limitation set on the size of Newburyport ships by the depth of water over the bar at the harbor mouth. The East India trade demanded larger ships than Newburyport could furnish, so Salem and Portsmouth were able to develop this important trade at the expense of the town on the Merrimack.

While there are interesting buildings in all parts of the town, the chief architectural interest of Newburyport lies in its High Street, which, wide and straight, and shaded by elm trees throughout its length of three miles, is one of the most charming streets to be found anywhere in New England. It lies along "The Ridge," a gentle rise of land roughly parallel to the river, and many of the old houses on its upper side stand on terraces well above the street and have deep gardens behind them running back to pasture and farm land beyond. A most interesting view of the town may be had from the rear of some of the places on the upper side of the High Street. Many of the gardens have in them little arbors or summer houses of latticework, that are as old as the houses themselves. Several of the more important gardens, especially those that are terraced, are of considerable interest and charm. One passing through the town is impressed by the large number of great, square three-storied houses whose dignified aspect testifies to the prosperity and good taste of their builders of a hundred years ago and more. The houses of this type were built, for the most part, between the Revolution and the War of 1812,

around which were ranged on high pedestals a number of wooden statues representing George Washington, Benjamin Franklin, John Hancock and other historical worthies, together with several mythological characters and a number of animals.

While houses of the square, three-storied type are undoubtedly what give its predominant character to the town, there are notable examples of the two-storied gambrel-roof type as well, of which the Bradbury-Spalding House

JAMES NOYES HOUSE — 1646 — NEWBURY, MASSACHUSETTS
The doorways are additions made about 1830.

few of them antedating the Declaration of Independence. Among the earliest and finest of the houses of this type are the Lowell-Johnson House and the Jackson-Dexter House, both in the High Street. The latter house was the residence of that eccentric merchant who called himself "Lord" Timothy Dexter, around whose name various legends have accumulated, among them the story of a shipload of warmingpans sent to the West Indies, where they were sold at great profit as ladles for use in sugar refineries. An old print shows how this house looked in Timothy Dexter's time, when it had a sort of forecourt between it and the street,

in Green Street, built about 1790, is one of the best. Much older is the house in State Street now occupied by the Dalton Club. It is not known just when this was built, but its builder, Michael Dalton, bought the land in 1746, which would place the date of its erection later, at all events, than that. The boarding of the front is coursed in imitation of stone. The interior finish is very good and there is a particularly fine staircase with twisted newels and balusters. It was in this house that George Washington stayed when on his journey through the New England states. An unusual feature of this house is the great breadth of its facade,

JONATHAN PLUMMER HOUSE—1760—NEWBURY OLDTOWN, MASSACHUSETTS

which made it possible to have five dormers in the roof without any sense of crowding.

A still older type of two-storied house having a plain pitched roof is the Short House, at 6 High Street, Newbury, which was built soon after 1717, when the land was acquired by Nathaniel Knight, and is given an unusual character by the large square chimney in each gable, the gable ends of the house being of brick. The front door of this house is of a kind unusual in that part of the country, with its pair of doors and the narrow light over them.

in quite high relief, and carrying carved brackets which support the pediment.

In Newbury and Oldtown and the outlying portions of Newburyport are numerous farmhouses of the simple and dignified type found almost everywhere in New England, but the individual character of Newburyport is chiefly given by the square three-storied "Mansion Houses," of which so many are found in the High Street.

Newburyport, although today manufacturing has taken the place of seaborne commerce as its

"LORD" TIMOTHY DEXTER HOUSE—c1772—NEWBURYPORT, MASSACHUSETTS
Showing the house as it at present stands after the removal of the forecourt and statues.

These doors are undoubtedly the original ones and are of interest on that account, as few existing outside doors in old houses are of the period of the house itself. In many cases, not only the doors, but their architectural framework as well, have been replaced by later ones much inferior in design and detail to the rest of the building, so that one often sees on houses that obviously date from the eighteenth century, doorways of the pseudo-Greek type of 1830.

In the neighboring town of Byfield, which was formerly Byfield parish of the town of Newbury, is the very interesting old house which is now the residence of the headmaster of Dummer Academy. Its main entrance is unlike any other in the neighborhood, its pilasters being ornamented with grapevines carved

chief industry, is less changed than most other old towns of its importance, and one can easily form a good idea of how it must have looked in the year 1800 when Timothy Dwight, President of Yale College, visited it while on a tour through the New England states, after which visit he wrote:

"The houses, taken collectively, make a better appearance than those of any other town in New England. Many of them are particularly handsome. Their appendages, also, are unusually neat. Indeed, an air of wealth, taste and elegance is spread over this beautiful spot with a cheerfulness and brilliancy to which I know no rival. . . . Upon the whole, few places probably in the world furnish more means of a delightful residence than Newburyport."

FOSTER HOUSE — 1808 — NEWBURYPORT, MASSACHUSETTS
Note the wide corner-boards, the interesting treatment of the deck and detail of the dormers

KNAPP-PERRY HOUSE — 1809 — 47 HIGH STREET, NEWBURYPORT, MASSACHUSETTS
The wooden fence corresponds in design with railing around the deck of the house.

BRADBURY-SPALDING HOUSE — 1790 — 28 GREEN STREET, NEWBURYPORT, MASSACHUSETTS
Built by Theophilus Bradbury. An especially good example of the gambrel roof, three-dormer type. The doorway has splayed jambs, a characteristic feature of Newburyport houses.

THOMAS HALE HOUSE, 348 HIGH STREET, NEWBURYPORT, MASSACHUSETTS
A very dignified three-story house. Both the porch and the fence are original.

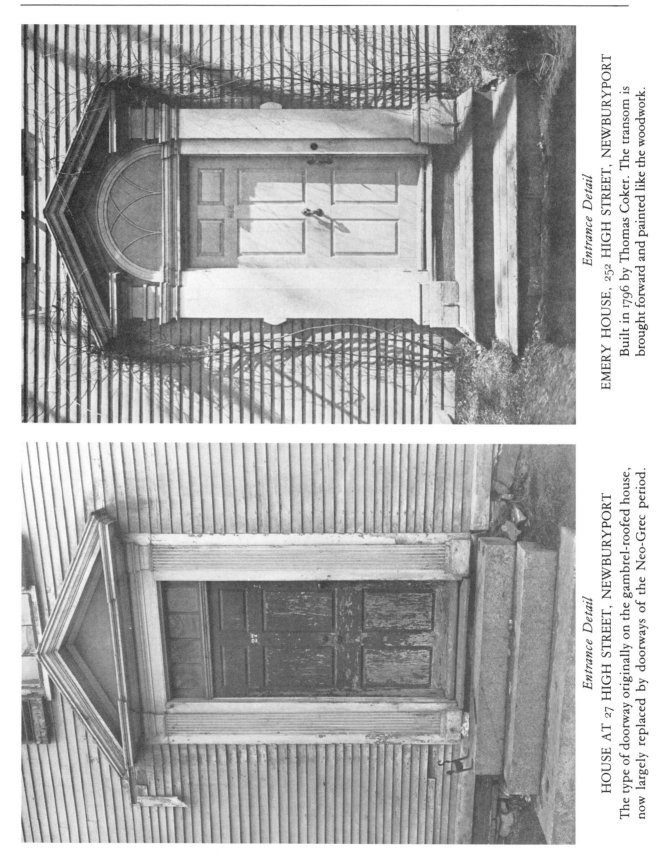

Entrance Detail

EMERY HOUSE, 252 HIGH STREET, NEWBURYPORT

Built in 1796 by Thomas Coker. The transom is brought forward and painted like the woodwork.

Entrance Detail

HOUSE AT 27 HIGH STREET, NEWBURYPORT

The type of doorway originally on the gambrel-roofed house, now largely replaced by doorways of the Neo-Grec period.

THOMAS HALE HOUSE—1800—348 High Street
The columns rest on round reeded pedestals.

Porch

STOREY-WALTERS HOUSE—1801—68 High Street
Built by Samuel Sweet.

MOULTON HOUSE — c1810 — NEWBURYPORT, MASSACHUSETTS
A stately example of the three-story Newburyport house.
The houses along the Ridge are of similar type.

SAWYER-HALE HOUSE, NEWBURYPORT, MASSACHUSETTS
Built during the latter part of the eighteenth century. Particularly
good cornice, dormer spacing, and broken scroll pediment.

SHORT HOUSE — 1717 — NEWBURY, MASSACHUSETTS

A two-storied house of the older type with plain pitched roof and large square chimney in each gable end.

Detail of Doorway
SHORT HOUSE — 1717 — NEWBURY, MASSACHUSETTS
These are among the oldest paneled doors in New England.

Early Dwellings of Nantucket

Text by
J. A. Schweinfurth

Photographs by
Julian A. Buckly
Originally published in 1917 as White Pine Monograph
Volume III, Number 6

MANSION, CORNER OF MAIN AND PLEASANT STREETS, NANTUCKET

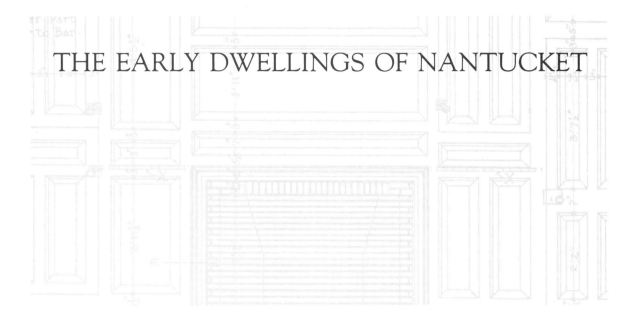

THE EARLY DWELLINGS OF NANTUCKET

ON the diamond-leaded panes of the windows in a certain ancient manor house in old England, one reads this inscription:

GOD
BY THIS MEANS
HATH SENT
WHAT I ON THIS
HOUSE HAVE SPENT

and:

ALL PRAYSE BE UNTO HIS
NAME THAT GAVE ME
MEANS TO BUILD THE SAME
1 6 3 8

This is accompanied by a couple of screws of tobacco and several pipes—indicating that tobacco did it.

On this quaint old island of Nantucket, all that is left to indicate the source of the one time wealth which built the fine old houses and mansions, are the numerous weather vanes bearing a whale, "right" or "sperm," which appear in the most unexpected places, giving an unmistakable local color to many a very interesting vista. There is, also, the characteristic "Captain's Walk"—a simple balustraded platform supported on posts resting on the sides of the gabled roofs, built to obtain a view of incoming and outgoing vessels. For in those days a whaling cruise often lasted years, and the homecoming was a matter of the very greatest interest to all. If one looks through the collection of the Nantucket Historical Society, and studies certain musty old volumes in Nantucket's most admirably conducted Public Library, there will

gradually emerge certain historical facts explaining the peculiar character which distinguishes the colonial work here, from that existing anywhere else.

Nantucket was from its earliest days an Atlantic outpost far from the mainland. Its people, who were mostly English, from their very isolation became an independent, self-sufficient folk, almost a law unto themselves. More than one commission was sent from the mainland to set them right with their colonial Governors who claimed authority over them. Quakerism was brought over from England, and from that time on the history of Nantucket is the story of the rise and fall of the Quakers. These people, so named according to Fox, the eminent English missionary of their sect, because at the mention of their Maker's name every one should tremble, were at first a simple folk, making much of personal liberty and man's natural rights, which, however, did not keep them from owning slaves both red and black; nor, while strongly advocating temperance, prevent them from taking intoxicating drinks. Adopting forms of speech designed to be a protest against caste, they did not protest against such caste. "While they ruled, it was like unto the days of Noah—all Quakers were safe within the Ark, and all outsiders were drowned in a Sea of Sin."

Many joined their church because they paid no salaries to their preachers, and their meeting-houses were of the simplest style, free from all ostentation, as were their laws; the dues, therefore, were light, and these characteristics naturally were reflected in their simple, plain architecture. It is this simplicity of form, this absence of small and enriched detail, together with a simple but well-proportioned mass, with a mastery of the "fourth dimension,"—things which did not cost a great deal of money, but which did require some expenditure of thought—that impress one today as he wanders through the weed-grown streets, which are bathed in such brilliant sunlight as one gets only on a sunny day at sea; for this island is anchored thirty miles out at sea, with the Gulf Stream only sixty miles away. Standing on the boisterous beach at 'Sconset, looking over the tumultuous breakers toward the East, the nearest land is Spain.

tain rule-of-thumb following of Greek precedent, influenced by hands and hearts which have builded many ships; a certain tightness, of ship-shapeness; newel posts, rails, etc., suggest the crude but strong and rugged work of the ship's carpenter. They look as if they had weathered many a salty storm and stress, and yet inexpensive—there is no ostentatious display. As Quakerism declined, and fortunes began to be made rapidly in whalebone and oil, the wealthy "Sea Captains" built more imposing mansions, such as the two porticoed houses on Main Street at the corner of Pleasant Street—two veritable

TWO HOUSES IN MAIN STREET, NANTUCKET

The one nearer, the Kent House, is, all things considered, one of the best of the small houses in Nantucket, with typical doorway; it has the clean-cut, chaste effect of Greek work, and is totally devoid of all effort. The body of the house is a beautiful warm gray, the finish white; it is remarkably well kept up by a very appreciative owner.

The accompanying illustrations give clearly a suggestion of the strong clear light and deep transparent shadow on sun-flecked clapboards, cornice and doorway of many of the houses. There are the simplest expedients adopted to obtain these shadows—for example, one often finds over a door or window a seven eighths of an inch board projecting about four inches, often with no bed mould, giving just the right projection for an effective shadow. There is a cer-

classic temples in white pine—one in the Greek, the other in the Roman feeling.

In Nantucket's palmy days it ranked third in the list of the wealthiest towns of Massachusetts—after Boston and Salem. Her churches, "built out of full pockets and with willing hearts," were well filled with solid wealthy men. The Unitarians were said to be "so wealthy that they could have built their churches of mahogany, and gilded them all over."

HOUSE IN MAIN STREET, NANTUCKET

A simple, unobtrusive, typical white house in a village street, with hardly any detail, all bathed in sparkling sunlight and splashed with purple-gray shadow; it makes a picture long to be remembered.

MARIA MITCHELL HOUSE — 1790 — VESTAL STREET, NANTUCKET

Birthplace of the great astronomer — one of the famous women of America.
This shows a good example of the "Captain's Walk" on the roof.

"DUTCH CAP" HOUSE IN MAIN STREET, NANTUCKET
Known as the Bucknam House.

These were the times when Nantucket counted in the affairs of the great world. Its bold seamen, its enterprising and skillful merchants and whale hunters brought to it fame and fortune. Earlier in its history it had sent to England with a cargo of oil, etc., the two vessels, the *Beaver* and the *Dartmouth*. Loaded with tea, they sailed on the return voyage to Boston, where was held the historic Boston Tea Party. All but a very few chests of tea were thrown

Square a few steps down a quiet weedy little lane, there nestles a discreet doorway with the legend "Somerset Club" over its chaste portal.

In the rooms of the Nantucket Historical Society, among the relics testifying to this Island's past greatness, one may read the very interesting log books of the bold whale hunters. These are often quaintly illustrated—sometimes with the number of whales taken on the day of entry, each drawn out in solid black. A few extracts

HOUSE ON ACADEMY HILL

Known as the Captain Roland Gardner House. A brilliant white house with deep green blinds and surrounded with very dark green foliage, giving a very opulent color effect.

overboard. The remaining ones were taken by the Captains to Nantucket, and disposed of advantageously and with some discretion. This is the tradition as set forth by some of the descendants of these "Sea Cap'ns," sitting about the huge coal stove set in a circular sawdust arena, protected by a gas-pipe foot-rest, in the center of the "Captains' Room" in the ancient Rotch Building at the lower end of the Town Square. Just opposite is the very exclusive Union Club, which boasts of its works of art. And across the

from the Sea Journal of Peleg ("Pillick") Folger will give an illuminating sidelight on the character of these men. It will be inferred that "Pillick" was what is known in our times as a "good sport"—quoting consoling or congratulatory texts, according to whether the day was a profitable one or not.

"July 1st. Nantucket bears N.E. 324 miles. We had a good breakfast upon meat and doboys & we are all merry together. A

GRISCOM MANSION, CORNER OF FAIR AND MAIN STREETS, NANTUCKET

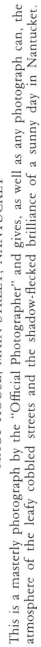

MACY HOUSE, MAIN STREET, NANTUCKET

This is a masterly photograph by the "Official Photographer" and gives, as well as any photograph can, the atmosphere of the leafy cobbled streets and the shadow-flecked brilliance of a sunny day in Nantucket.

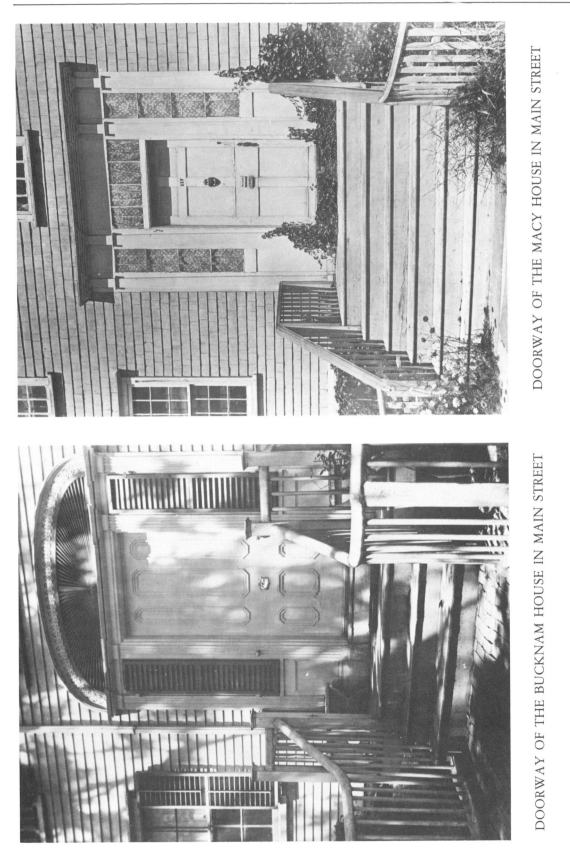

DOORWAY OF THE MACY HOUSE IN MAIN STREET

DOORWAY OF THE BUCKNAM HOUSE IN MAIN STREET

TWO OF THE FAMOUS DOORWAYS OF NANTUCKET

slippery kind of breeze—only we wish we could get some spermaceti."

"July 8th. This day we spy'd Spermacetis & we kill'd one. If we get whale enough we may be able to go home in a fortnight. 'Death Summons all men to the silent grave.'"

"July 9th. Lat. 36–18 Longt. 73–0. Nothing remarkable this 24 hours only dull times and Hot weather & no whales to be seen. Much toil and labour mortal man is

And after hard weather and no whales:

"And so one day passeth after another & every Day brings us nearer to our Grave and all human employments will be at an end."

This Island during its long career suffered many disasters at home as well as in its ventures on the far seas. On a fine midsummer day in the year 1846, as usual, the coopers, spar makers,

DYER HOUSE, NUMBER 9 MILK STREET, NANTUCKET

This is one of the most interesting houses in the town and is remarkable for its color and proportion. In rambler rose season there is a mass of crimson and green against a background of pinkish gray with white finish. This house is owned by some very appreciative "off-islanders" and has been kept up with a great deal of loving care.

forced to endure & little profit to be got out of it."

.   .   .   .

"and we struck a large Spermaceti and killed her . . . and we hoisted her head about 2 foot above water and then we cut a scuttle in her head, and a man got in up to his Armpits and dipt almost 6 Hogsheads of clear Oyle out of her case besides 6 more out of her Noddle. He certainly doth but the right that mingles profit and delight."

riggers, sail makers, and iron smiths were making harpoons, lances and knives, the cordage factories turning out ropes and rigging—all noisily plying their trades—the busy wharves alive with the loading of stores and unloading of cargoes of oil, and the huge drays rumbling over the cobbles with their great casks of sperm oil or huge bundles of whalebone bound for the commodious warehouses. Now the great bell in the Old South belfry booms out an alarm; the great fire which is to mark the decline of the town's prosperity is raging. The intense heat from the burning burst the casks and hogsheads of oil, and their fiery contents spread a burning flood

DOORWAY IN QUINCE STREET, NANTUCKET

The body of the house is a light gray with white finish. The door is of the most vivid emerald green with a brass latch; the lattice supporting a rambler rose bush and with a golden door-mat on a rose pink brick sidewalk makes a riot of brilliant color.

mometer reaches 100° and over, make it a favorite retreat for nervous invalids and seekers after sleep and rest.

The residents say that many of the fine houses were taken apart and transported by schooners to the mainland, and there re-erected—some landing in the vicinity of New York City. The white pine used almost exclusively in these houses is said by some to have come from Maine, which is not far away, by others to have grown on the Island; and they point to huge rotting stumps sometimes unearthed in certain wet places about the Island.

Most of the doors used were of but two panels—and sometimes one—the panels being in one piece often over twenty-five inches wide. In the Maria Mitchell House there is a white pine door three feet wide and six feet high and about one inch thick, painted white, made up of two pieces, one piece being twenty-seven inches wide, standing perfectly free from warping, and fitted with fine wrought-iron strap hinges, and a massive polished mahogany latch and fittings, giving to this white door an air of elegance, and all no doubt the work of some good old ship carpenter.

PORCH OF ONE OF THE EARLY EIGHTEENTH-CENTURY HOUSES OF NANTUCKET.

Showing peculiar cornice with heavy consoles simply sawed out of white pine planks.

over the harbor. In twenty-four hours the flames swept clean an area of thirty-six acres in the center of the town, impoverishing more than two hundred families.

After this blow, from which the town never recovered, the use of lard oil for illuminating began to be popular, and the recently discovered mineral oils of Pennsylvania brought a flood of oil which completely submerged the whale oil industry. So the business of whaling, in which so much of the capital of the people was invested, declined rapidly. The more enterprising men left for the mainland—some for California in the Gold Rush of 1849. The last whaling ship left the port in 1869. In time, a stranded ship and a poor old widow were quoted as fit emblems of this quaint old seaport town.

Its population of real Nantucketers of about three thousand is swelled in a good season by from seven to ten thousand "off-islanders," among these being many seekers after health; its peculiar breezes which blow all day long, its sea air and its mild and fairly stable temperature of not over 82°, while on the mainland the ther-

Doorway and Cornice
LITTLE HOUSE ON ACADEMY HILL, NANTUCKET

While the photographer was proceeding without haste to "get" this house, the owner, in carpet slippers and shirt sleeves, appeared, and with some show of feeling inquired: "Now what *is* the matter of this house? All you fellows are photographing it and drawing it and sketching it and measuring it. *What is it?*" "It" was the moulded pilasters, the finely proportioned doorway, the cornice with its inexpensive but effective sawed tongues, and the lintels over the windows.

sonable in cost, compared with our massive two by four stud partition in these days of reckless waste. The plastering is uncommonly hard and durable. Though economical in most ways, the builders of those early days were lavish in the use of bricks, the chimneys usually being large and massive; and in the basement of old houses one often sees curious methods of brick arching and vaulting, the mortar used appearing to be a sort of light clay, crumbling to the touch, but having been serviceable for over a hundred years.

Nantucket's streets are quiet now. Many of its best houses are owned by "off-islanders" from far-away prosperous cities, who occupy them only in the vacation season. The hum of the busy shops is heard no more — and the deep rumble of the heavily laden dray with its huge hogsheads of oil bumping over the cobbled streets has given way to the rattle of the beach wagon with its summer visitors, passengers bound for the bathing beach or the melancholy ride across the somber moors, to where the huge rollers, after a journey of three thousand miles across the stormy Atlantic, break on this bleak and barren shore.

The sashes in this house are of white pine a scant inch in thickness, with muntins one inch wide enclosing panes of glass about six inches wide by eight and three-eighths inches high; the doors, in general, being about two feet four inches wide, and fifteen sixteenths of an inch thick, of two panels in height, — so it will be seen no pine was wasted.

The interior partitions were usually not supporting partitions, the floors being carried by heavy beams mortised into heavy girts, corner posts, etc., which were exposed and painted. The partitions were, therefore, mere curtains, being made of unplaned seven eighths inch pine boards, eight to ten inches wide, with two or three inches of space between each, set vertically and nailed at floor and ceiling. In this was worked the door frame and then it was lathed and plastered on both sides, making a perfectly durable partition for such low-studded rooms — not over two and three eighths inches thick, and withal very rea-

Entrance Porch
FOLGER HOUSE IN CENTER STREET,
NANTUCKET

Porch

MIXTER HOUSE ON ACADEMY HILL, NANTUCKET

This shows, besides some peculiarly grooved detail, the remarkable decorative effect of English ivy, which flourishes well in Nantucket, and day lily leaves against a clear warm gray clapboarded house. The white pine clapboards have a suggestion of a bead on their edge.

Marblehead: Its Contribution
to American Architecture

Text by
William Truman Aldrich

Photographs by
Julian A. Buckly
Originally published in 1918 as White Pine Monograph
Volume IV, Number 1

Detail of Entrance Porch

LEE MANSION, MARBLEHEAD, MASSACHUSETTS

Formerly the home of Col. Jeremiah Lee. This house is now in the possession of
the Marblehead Historical Society, and is filled with mementos of historical value.

MARBLEHEAD: ITS CONTRIBUTION TO EIGHTEENTH AND EARLY NINETEENTH CENTURY AMERICAN ARCHITECTURE

FROM the time of the earliest settlement in 1629 the townsmen of Marblehead, Massachusetts, have shown qualities, in times of hardship and stress, of a very high order. Wars, sickness, fires and storms have all at various times sorely tried this little community and have developed a people justly distinguished for their fortitude and courage. The daily familiarity with danger and suffering of the men in the fishing fleet made a splendid training for the part they were to play in the wars of the Revolution and of 1812, and the pride in this tradition of service was nobly sustained by the later generations in the time of the Civil War. Nor are the men of today one bit less patriotic and willing to do their share. Out of all proportion to its size and wealth has been Marblehead's contribution to the store of early American history and legend, and the names of many of its men and women are part of the country's best heritage.

Salem is but four miles away and of course has somewhat eclipsed in popular interest its smaller neighbor, and the splendor of its Colonial architecture of the early nineteenth century has appealed to the imagination of architects and laymen more strongly than the humbler dwellings of the nearby town. But there is a tremendous amount of material to be found on the hilly, rocky peninsula of Marblehead, not only to satisfy the seeker for picturesqueness and literary associations, but also for the study of early American architecture. While the peninsula which is called Marblehead is about four miles long and from two miles to a mile and a half wide, the town itself, where almost all the old buildings are to be found, is perhaps two miles long by half a mile wide and extends along the harbor side. The site is very hilly and irregular and the coastline very rocky. So the streets must needs wander about in a most delightfully casual way, and the houses must face every which way and the yards both back and front are necessarily restricted and form most charming terraces and gardens. The same characteristic steep streets descending to the water and tiers of houses rising above one another that have given Genoa and Naples and Quebec so much of their charm are here repeated on a smaller scale. The houses, while they are all free-standing, as befits this sturdy and independent people, are nevertheless built closely together for their mutual comfort and neighborliness. The irregularities of site have resulted in a greater variety of plan in many of the houses than can be met with in most of our New England communities, where the town sites are almost uniformly flat.

As seen from the harbor or from the causeway that connects Marblehead Neck with the mainland, the silhouette of the town presents a picture unrivalled in this country for beauty of skyline.

Abbot Hall, with its exceedingly graceful spire, was admirably designed and placed as a climax to the rising lines of the town. The shipping in the harbor (Marblehead is probably the most active yachting center in the country), the trees, and the wonderful variety of roofs and chimneys, all together make charming patterns within the long, harmonious contours of the hills.

like the House of Seven Gables in Salem, or the Cooper-Austin House in Cambridge, which immediately attracts the visitor's attention as an example of the earliest period of Colonial. By far the greatest number of dwellings date from the period of Marblehead's greatest prosperity, the middle of the eighteenth century.

The Revolution took a heavy toll of Marble-

HOUSE ON THE SEA FRONT, MARBLEHEAD, MASSACHUSETTS

Back of this austere old house appears a bit of Marblehead's
harbor, which is one of the finest along the New England shore.

There is no New England town which shows so many old houses in a single *coup d'oeil.*

The most prevalent type of house is the wooden clapboard one with gable or gambrel roof and generous brick chimneys. Even the more pretentious houses on Washington Street are of wood; in fact, there are only five or six old houses to be found that are built of brick. While there are several houses dating from before 1700, there is not one whose exterior aspect remains in a form typical of the seventeenth century, and not one

head's resources in wealth of men and money, and we find few examples of the later period of McIntire and after.

Although the houses near Abbot Hall and on Washington Street are large and in a sense pretentious, and the Lee Mansion is one of the finest mansions in New England of its period, in general it is the homes of people of modest and humble circumstances that leave the most permanent impress on the memory of the observer. Even the richer houses are almost entirely de-

FRANKLIN STREET, MARBLEHEAD, MASSACHUSETTS

Showing the way in which the houses are generally built on the street line.

HOUSE ON STATE STREET, MARBLEHEAD, MASSACHUSETTS

BOWEN HOUSE, MARBLEHEAD, MASSACHUSETTS

One of the oldest houses in the town. It is situated on the corner of Mugford
Street near the Town House. A glimpse is afforded of the irregularity of the land.

void of carved ornaments and any elaboration of detail. In a word, austerity is the distinguishing characteristic of building in Marblehead.

But it must not be thought that bareness and monotony are the necessary accompaniments of this very democratic simplicity so expressive of what we like to think is or was the best side of American character. I believe nowhere will there be found more varieties of gables, cornices

boast of exceedingly effective cupolas and the Col. Jeremiah Lee Mansion is embellished with a pediment on its main façade. Otherwise the roofs of Marblehead are of a soul-satisfying simplicity; even dormers are a great rarity, the few there are being later additions, with the exception of the house on Mechanic Street shown in the illustration on page 88. These three rather heavily moulded dormers in the gambrel roof are probably of the same date as the house. There are,

"KING" HOOPER HOUSE, MARBLEHEAD, MASSACHUSETTS

Formerly the residence of "The Honorable Robert Hooper, Esq.," one of the wealthiest merchants of New England before the Revolution. "King" Hooper, as he was called, lived in princely style for those days. Some of the highest dignitaries of the land were entertained in the large banquet hall in the third story.

and doorways, or better examples of interior finish and paneling.

The gambrel roofs vary in angles from very steep and narrow to certain examples of low, wide gambrels, where one wonders how the flatter pitches can be kept from leaking. In the same way a designer may find precedent for gable roofs from twenty degrees all the way up to sixty degrees inclination. There are very few hipped roofs. The two Lee houses both

on the most interesting old Governor Bradford House in Bristol, Rhode Island, three dormers in a gambrel roof that are almost identical in size and detail with the Marblehead examples, and both houses are of about the same date.

The verge boards up the rakes of the gables and gambrels are narrow and kept close in to the clapboards with only a slight moulding at the edge of the shingles. This lack of raking cornice or projection gives a distinction to all the

HOUSE ON MECHANIC STREET, MARBLEHEAD, MASSACHUSETTS
Dormer windows are unusual in Marblehead, and lend additional interest to this subject.

LEE MANSION —1768 — MARBLEHEAD, MASSACHUSETTS

Built by Col. Jeremiah Lee. Its original cost is said to have been ten thousand pounds. It is still noted for its excellent hall and stairway.

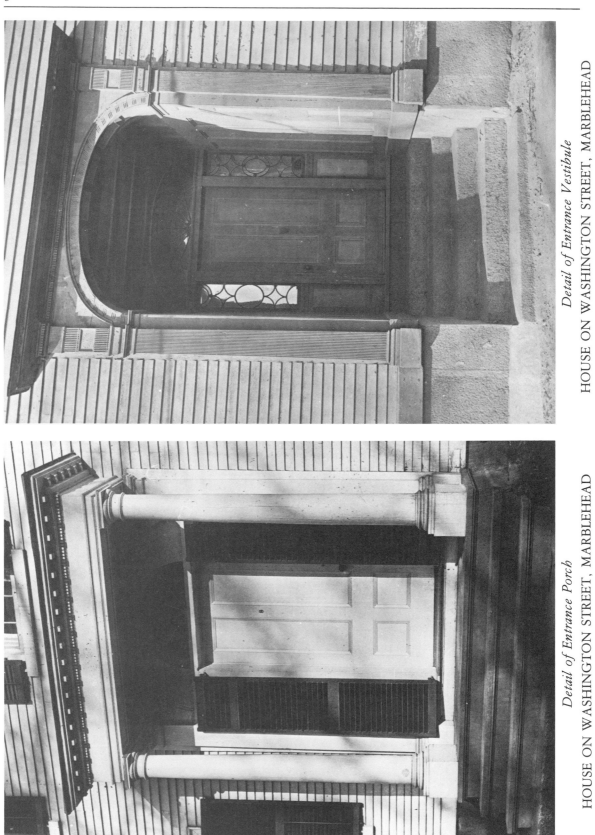

Detail of Entrance Vestibule

HOUSE ON WASHINGTON STREET, MARBLEHEAD

Detail of Entrance Porch

HOUSE ON WASHINGTON STREET, MARBLEHEAD

HOUSE ON WASHINGTON STREET, MARBLEHEAD, MASSACHUSETTS

HOUSE ON TUCKER STREET, MARBLEHEAD, MASSACHUSETTS

Doorway
HOUSE ON FRANKLIN STREET MARBLEHEAD,
MASSACHUSETTS
It appears that the hall wainscoting cap has been repeated on
the pilasters on the outside of the main entrance.

in years gone by, and they can be most profitably studied by modern designers.

The Doric order was evidently invented for Marblehead, as all but two or three of the front entrances are adorned with it in the form of column or pilaster. The two Lee houses flaunt the gay Ionic, and on Franklin Street there are two extraordinary doorways of the early nineteenth century flanked by delightfully quaint pilasters of a curious composite type, tapering downward to their plinths. Especially interesting, too, is the enclosed entrance porch on a house in Lookout Court, with its elliptical fanlight, reeded pilasters and grooved ornaments. So many of the houses are built on the sidewalk line that there are many interesting examples of recessed doorways with the steps in the recess. The illustration shows an excellent early nineteenth-century one. Most characteristic are the various treatments of outside steps made necessary by the steep grades met with everywhere.

The interiors of these alluring houses are fully as interesting as the exteriors. No good American should fail to see the truly exquisite rooms and the wonderful staircase of the Lee Mansion,

roofs which is lost by any designer who departs from it.

The older cornices are simple as can be, and are without any decorative feature; but later there is a fascinating variety of moulded cornices with dentils and modillions all worthy of careful study. What a lesson this town teaches in the value of cornices of small projection and few members.

Clapboards cover the walls of almost every building, but we find several instances of wood boarding cut to imitate stone in a simple rusticated pattern, on all sides as on the Lee Mansion, and only on the front as on the "King" Hooper House. Corner boards are the rule, varying from four to eight inches in width.

The exterior window trims vary greatly and are of great interest. In many cases the second-story trims are charmingly composed with the bed mouldings of the cornice. Often the first-story windows have little cornices of their own. The very satisfying quality of the window sashes and blinds is due to careful thought by some one

Entrance Porch
HOUSE ON WASHINGTON STREET, MARBLEHEAD,
MASSACHUSETTS

Doorway
GENERAL JOHN GLOVER HOUSE—1762—
MARBLEHEAD, MASSACHUSETTS
The home of the famous Revolutionary general.

according to tradition, rowed Washington across the Delaware River on that famous wintry night, December 25th, 1776. Read the real story of Skipper Ireson, that much maligned seaman, whom Whittier immortalized in the same poem in which the women of Marblehead are unjustly given the role of avenging furies. Poor Ireson! He was given the ride on the rail in the tarry and feathery coat, but not by the women of Marblehead. The perpetrators of this outrage were fishermen of the town whose indignation had been aroused by the stories of the crew of Ireson's schooner, who had forced him against his will to abandon the other craft in distress. Ireson's crew were at fault and shifted the blame to their skipper when the story came out. Learn how completely American a Massachusetts town has been and always will be. Just imagine—the curfew tolls every evening at nine and the boys and girls celebrate Guy Fawkes day every November fifth with bonfires and a procession!

which is without a peer in this country. Nor should he fail to see the "King" Hooper House, to appreciate the wholesome beauty of the second-period paneling and fireplaces of this fine example.

There are other buildings in town of special interest—the old Town House, the Powder House of 1750, and the Old North Church, each worthy of a visit, as is the burial ground, to remind us of the frailty of us humans and of the fact that our forefathers used to make better lettering than we do.

By all means, gentle reader, visit Marblehead, and you will profit greatly thereby; spend at least a day if a layman, and at least a week if you are an architect. Read up in Mr. Road's History the stories of Mugford the brave sailor who captured the British transport *Hope* when in command of the American schooner *Franklin*, of Agnes Surriage and Sir John Frankland, of Gerry and Storey, of the gallant General Glover and his regiment, whose soldiers,

Entrance Porch
COL. WILLIAM R. LEE MANSION,
MARBLEHEAD, MASSACHUSETTS
Like the Col. Jeremiah Lee Mansion, this house is also surmounted by a cupola. The parlor was elaborately decorated by an Italian artist.

Detail of Entrance
HOUSE IN LOOKOUT COURT, MARBLEHEAD, MASSACHUSETTS
The elliptical fanlight and reeded pilasters give to this very old house a distinct architectural character.

Old Marblehead,
Part One

Text by
Frank Chouteau Brown

Photographs by
Arthur C. Haskell
Originally published in 1938 as White Pine Monograph
Volume XXIV, Number 2

View Along Hooper Street, Looking West
"KING" HOOPER MANSION—1745—MARBLEHEAD, MASSACHUSETTS

OLD MARBLEHEAD, MASSACHUSETTS
PART ONE

THE original settlement of Salem included within its area land now divided between Beverly, Peabody, Wenham, Manchester, Danvers, and Marblehead. It also covered Middleton, and parts of Topsfield and Essex. Marblehead itself was settled about 1629, although there exists a local tradition that its first resident was a man named Doliber, who came from the original group occupying Salem—then known as Naumkeag—previous to the arrival of Capt. John Endecott in June of 1628.

This legend extends into certain ramifying details that establish the site of his occupancy as one of the coves on or near Peach's Point,—and the form of his original residence as a fish hogshead!

Whether this be fact or fable, this convenient harbor was immediately appreciated by these early fisherfolk,—and by 1629, at least, it had begun to develop as a fishing village, at first called Nanepashemet—from the chief of the Naumkeag tribe of Indians who were found residing in the Salem area by the first English settlers. History—or, it still may be, legend—persists in claiming the original inhabitants who settled these rocky headlands, as fishermen from the islands of Guernsey and Jersey, in the British Channel, just off the coast of France.

The first Meeting House was located on the top of the steep, rocky elevation known as Old Burying Hill; still one of the highest sites in the town, with a number of protected coves lying near its base, and Beacon Hill just beyond. The picturesque little section of "Barnegat," with its pebbled beach crowded with fishing shacks, lobster pots, drying nets, and floats, and drawn-up dories nearby—still remains as a picture of the life that probably then—and for a hundred years and more thereafter—abounded in the little coves about the original church site, where the first Meeting House may have been built as early as 1638. From the Burying Hill you can still look down upon the placid landlocked waters of Little Harbor—with Gerry's Island only a few yards off

shore,—reached over a sand bar at low tide—where the first minister of the town, Parson William Walton dwelt from 1638 to 1668.

On one of the headlands of Peach's Point adjoining, stood the "Mr. Craddock's House" of which Winthrop wrote in his Journal, in September of 1633, "Mr. Craddock's House at Marblehead was burned down at midnight before, there being in it Mr. Allerton and many fishermen whom he employed that season, who were all preserved by a special providence of God, with most of his goods there, by a tailor, who sat up that night at work in the house, and hearing a noise, looked out and saw the house on fire above the oven in the thatch." This was the Isaac Allerton of Plymouth Colony, who was probably in Marblehead as early as 1629,—and may have been carrying on his enterprises in partnership with Craddock, who was the first London governor of the Massachusetts Company and was actively engaged in the fishing business.

From Marblehead was launched the third vessel built in the Colony, called the *Desire*, which returned from one of her early voyages to the West Indies, with the first cargo of slaves introduced into New England. Marblehead was named a "plantation" in 1635, and set apart from Salem in 1649; being incorporated by act of the General Court on May 2nd of that year.

The town originally grew up about the occasional fishermen's shacks, scattered irregularly upon the infrequent levels of the cliffs along the harbor, or clustered upon the few beaches to be found here and there at their base.

There could obviously not have been much order or regularity in such a Topsy-like growth as must have followed along this irregular shore. The first shacks were gradually replaced with small houses of two or three rooms, set any-which-way, wherever a small bit of level ground could be found, beside the paths that meandered up and down the rocky hillsides. Later, streets roughly paralleling the harbor line developed precariously; Front, backed again by Washington Street; with only one fairly level and straight street connecting them; State, leading from the Town Landing up to the old Town Square.

As, gradually, the old paths climbing the bluffs were superseded, wherever it was possible (though many still remain!) by wider twisting but still tortuously narrow ways; the little houses were partly turned about, had new rooms and fronts added, or—as was the case with the "King" Hooper building—an entirely new portion was built in 1745 to face the street,

the identical old site where first it took root. But Marblehead, dour in the stubbornness and content in the ignorance of its "98 per cent American ancestry," has thrown away no less than *three* opportunities to preserve its old picturesqueness! Its first settlement, about Fort Sewall and Little Harbor, had moved southwestward by 1700 to 1750 to a newer Town Square a full half mile; and this was, by a hundred and fifty years later, again abandoned for the still newer business center now at Washington and Atlantic Avenue,—but its too canny inhabitants, over three

OLD TOWN SQUARE, MARBLEHEAD, MASSACHUSETTS
Photograph taken in 1926 before the removal of Waters House and Bakery (1683) at the left

against one end of the older gambrel house that still backs it. In the case of the Capt. Samuel Trevett House, this was crowded in on the northeastern side of wandering Washington Street, well out upon the roadway, with its back against the higher rocky bluff, upon which a small doorway opens from the lower terrace of a crowding garden, from the upper levels of which one can almost see the harbor over the house!

It is not often a New England town is given three chances to retain its original identity, undisturbed— as usually it has to reproduce its integral parts upon

hundred years, have lacked entirely the business acumen and common sense to conserve its greatest asset and charm, the individual and historic character of its old-time glamour,—that might have been kept for all time, with no interruption in its business development and modern growth,—which still continues, faster and ranker, to the south and west!

But, besides the old Town Square, here shown, with its wooden Town House of 1727, as it appeared before the left hand group of buildings was demolished in 1937; it is still possible to find—here and there—an

Entrance Detail
OLD TOWN HALL—1727—TOWN SQUARE, MARBLEHEAD, MASSACHUSETTS

LEE STREET, LOOKING EAST,
MARBLEHEAD, MASSACHUSETTS

old street or a cluster of buildings; a weathered Fish House or Fisherman's Cottage; old Boat Shop, or remaining Boat Yard. But they all are passing fast. With the construction of a new sewer, some five and six years ago, there vanished almost instantly a whole flock of privies, that had for generations perched here and there, higglety-pigglety, about the back and side yards of the town, at all heights and angles—wherever a promising declivity or rock fissure could be found! And with them vanished no small part of the old-town atmosphere,—though here and there about the harbor there remain evanescent flavors of the old fish flakes and dressing grounds to attract the gulls—and cats!—as well as the visiting firemen and rich westerners in search of historic cultural American backgrounds!

In many old house interiors, where the paneled fireplace ends show sloping ceilings to the side walls, there has been a belief that they were originally built in that manner to simulate the curving lines of ship-cabins. This may actually have been occasionally the case; but it nevertheless is the fact that this type of interior appearance is not confined exclusively to the coast, as rooms of this character are often found on sites located at considerable distances from the ocean. It is, further, undoubtedly the fact, that many of these effects are accidental, while the floors have sub-

sided, the chimney and hearth have been kept up by their masonry support, so that the hearth slopes off from the underfire, along with the floor; or the underfire or hearth remains raised, often some inches above the floor level at sides and front, where floor slopes away from it, and down toward the two side walls.

In the Hooper House northwest second floor front bedroom, this effect appears—but the difference in level can hardly be over one and a half to two inches, and the floor slopes as well from the hearth to both sides, and from the fireplace wall toward the front of the room. In the other chamber it is more marked, the difference being at least three to four inches, but again it appears on both the floor and ceiling of this room, though it is not apparent upon the floor above.

In the Trevett House, these differences are still more marked. In both upper front rooms, the slopes show in the ceiling, more in the room on the eastern than the western side of the hall—but in both cases there exists evidence of the floor having had a similar unevenness at least partially corrected—showing in the bases beside the hearth in the eastern room, and in a raised underfire and hearth in the room across the hall.

In the first floor west side room (page 108) there is a 14 inch soffit under the beam forming part of the

GLOVER COURT, LOOKING NORTH,
MARBLEHEAD, MASSACHUSETTS

OLD HOUSES ON WASHINGTON STREET, LOOKING SOUTHEAST FROM TRAINING FIELD,
MARBLEHEAD, MASSACHUSETTS

OLD HOUSES ON FRANKLIN STREET, LOOKING NORTHEAST, MARBLEHEAD, MASSACHUSETTS

South Elevation — Older Rear Portion
"KING" HOOPER MANSION, MARBLEHEAD, MASSACHUSETTS

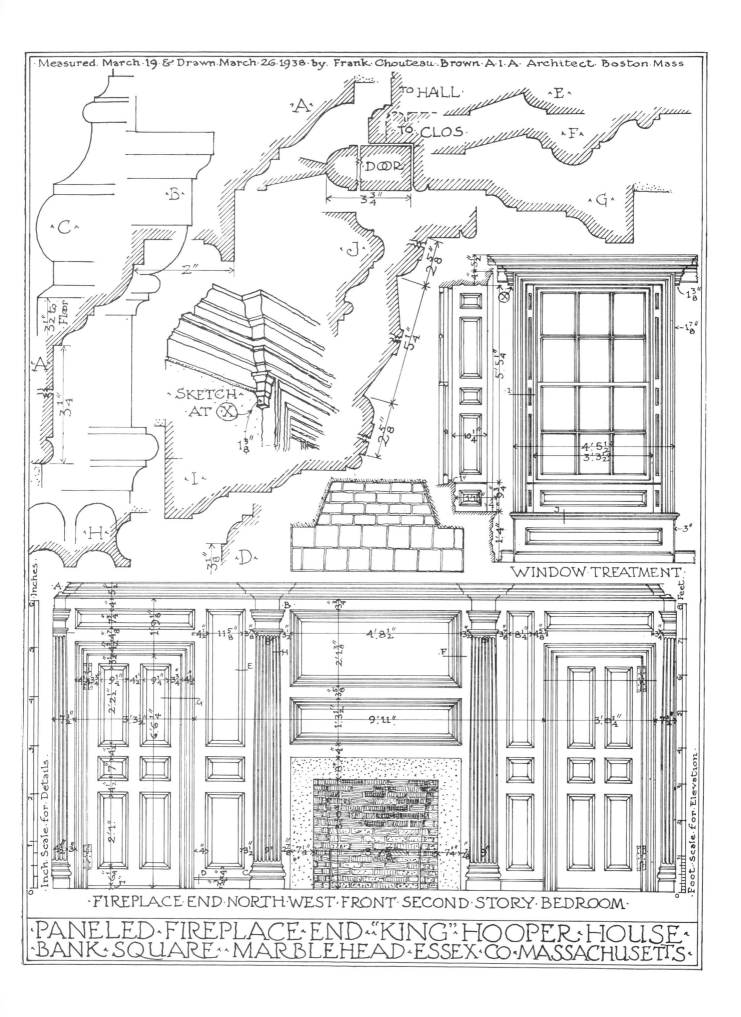

Measured. March. 19 & Drawn. March. 26. 1938. by. Frank. Chouteau. Brown. A.I.A. Architect. Boston. Mass

·A· ·E·
TO HALL ·F·
TO CLOS
·B· DOOR
·C· 3¾"
·J· ·G·

SKETCH AT (X)

WINDOW TREATMENT

·FIREPLACE·END·NORTH·WEST·FRONT·SECOND·STORY·BEDROOM·

·PANELED·FIREPLACE·END· "KING" ·HOOPER·HOUSE·
·BANK·SQUARE·MARBLEHEAD·ESSEX·CO·MASSACHUSETTS·

Fireplace End—Northwest Second Story Front Bedroom

Fireplace End—Southwest Second Story Front Bedroom
"KING" HOOPER MANSION—1745—MARBLEHEAD, MASSACHUSETTS

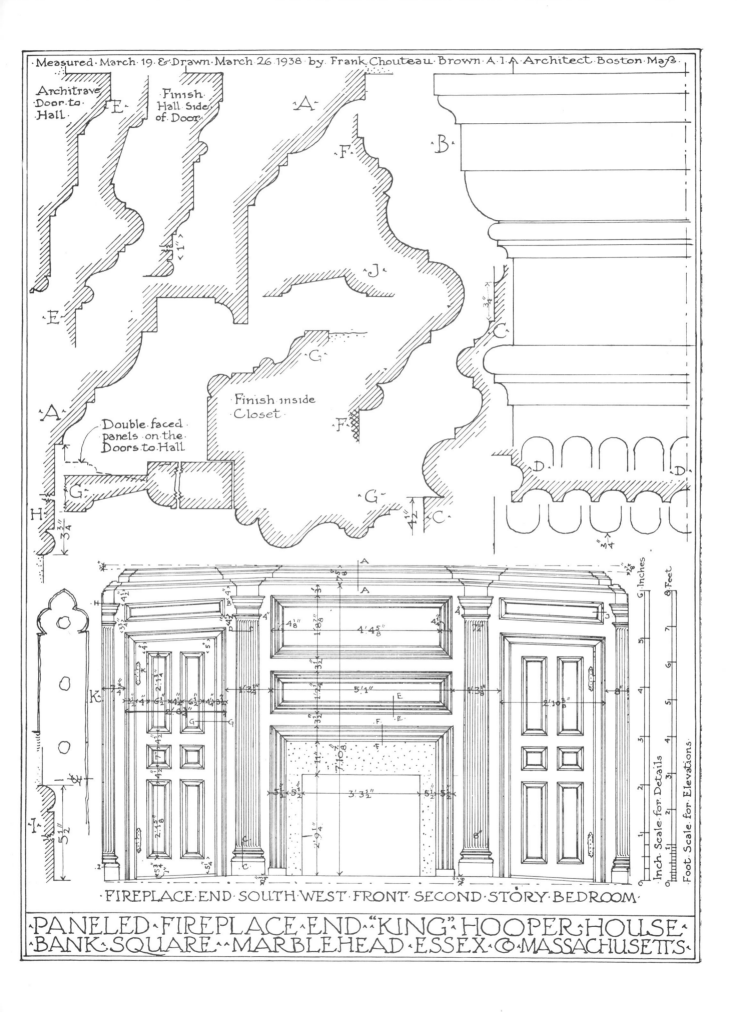

Measured·March·19·&·Drawn·March·26·1938·by·Frank·Chouteau·Brown·A·I·A·Architect·Boston·Mass·

Architrave Door to Hall

Finish Hall Side of Door

Double faced panels on the Doors to Hall

Finish inside Closet

FIREPLACE·END·SOUTH·WEST·FRONT·SECOND·STORY·BEDROOM·

Inch·Scale·for·Details.

Foot·Scale·for·Elevations.

PANELED·FIREPLACE·END·"KING"·HOOPER·HOUSE·
·BANK·SQUARE··MARBLEHEAD·ESSEX·CO·MASSACHUSETTS·

View of Hall from First Floor—Northwest Front Room
"KING" HOOPER MANSION—1745—MARBLEHEAD, MASSACHUSETTS

First Floor—Northeast Rear Room
CAPT. SAMUEL TREVETT HOUSE—BEFORE 1750—WASHINGTON STREET, MARBLEHEAD

First Floor—East Front Room

First Floor—West Front Room

CAPT. SAMUEL TREVETT HOUSE—BEFORE 1750—MARBLEHEAD, MASSACHUSETTS

cornice back to the face of the fireplace paneling, its soffit slopes upward at least two to two and a half inches, including the warped mouldings of the bed-moulding, while in the east room a still wider plaster soffit, from its front edge, warps up at the center to meet the higher fireplace paneling at this point.

ceilings seem to be brought at the front — or opposite — walls of the rooms, to a nearly level line, — which persists along the major part of the side walls, as well. In other words, so far as these two houses provide examples of so-called Ship Rooms, in a distinctly seafaring community, there exists evidence to show that

Washington Street Elevation

CAPT. SAMUEL TREVETT HOUSE — BEFORE 1750 — MARBLEHEAD, MASSACHUSETTS

But in the room at the back (page 107) the beam crossing in front of the second floor hearth, while straight, exposes behind it, the under part of the arch of the second floor hearth, from each side of which the ceiling slopes sharply to the side walls, where it is lower by almost five inches! In all these rooms the plaster

these inequalities occurred through settlement or shrinkage of wood supports in contrast to the portion of the walls supported by the masonry of the chimney construction. Which does not disprove that there may still exist Ship Rooms, intentionally so finished, far from the tang and roar of the ocean!

OLD HOUSES OFF THE ROAD TO FORT SEWALL, MARBLEHEAD, MASSACHUSETTS

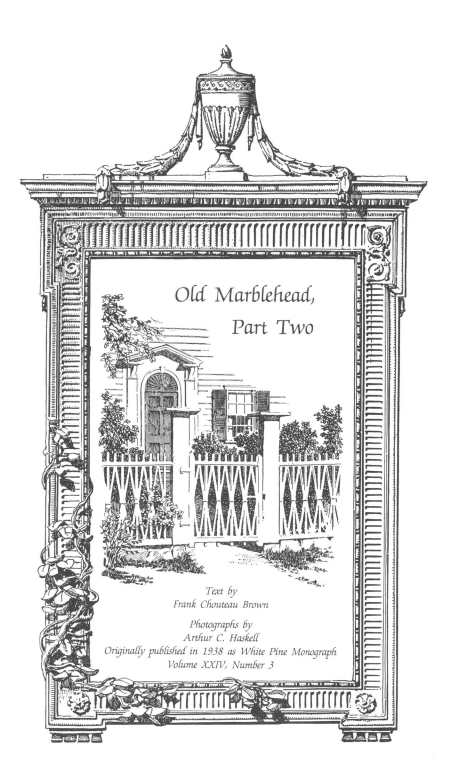

Old Marblehead,

Part Two

Text by
Frank Chouteau Brown

Photographs by
Arthur C. Haskell

Originally published in 1938 as White Pine Monograph
Volume XXIV, Number 3

Detail of Façade — New Portion (c1780)

COL. WILLIAM R. LEE HOUSE — 1745 — MARBLEHEAD, MASSACHUSETTS

OLD MARBLEHEAD, MASSACHUSETTS
PART TWO

ALTHOUGH the fine shelter provided by the Little Harbor at Marblehead (the larger anchorage lies open to gales from the northeast) was appreciated from the beginning by the fisherfolk from the English Channel Islands who were its first settlers; yet, despite their occasional increase by newcomers, probably from Lincolnshire, the growth of this portion of the Salem settlement seems to have been very slow. A nineteen-year-old graduate of Harvard College—Mr. John Cotton, a grandson of Cotton Mather—coming to teach at Marblehead about 1698, wrote in a letter of six years later, "When I came to this place—the whole township was not much bigger than a large farm, and very rocky, and so they are forc't to get their living out of the sea, not having room to confound the fisherman with the husbandman, and so spoil both as they do in some places. It has a very good Harbour which they improve to the best advantage for Fishing both Summer and Winter— And finally it is one of the best country places to keep school in, providing a man be firmly fix't in principles of virtue and religion, which I heartily wish were more abundant among them in the life and power of it."

There are various stories as to the derivation of the name of Marblehead. A quotation from a letter of the Rev. Francis Higgenson, written in 1629, is often given as its basis. He wrote, "here is plentie of marble-stone in such store that we have great rocks of it and a harbour nearby; our plantation is from thence called 'Marble Harbour' "—a name that shortly after appeared changed to Marblehead, possibly because of the number of adjoining headlands locally termed Heads—such as Goodwin's Head, Naugus Head.

After the death of the first Minister, Parson William Walton, in 1668, Mr. Samuel Cheever, an Harvard graduate was appointed, at 80 pounds the year (much of which he had to accept in merchandise— probably largely of fish!—on account of shortage of currency). This is known because of an existing town record, "resolved that 70% of Mr. Cheever's salary

should be paid in cash. Those refusing to pay in coin to have 25% added to their tax which is to be paid in good merchandise, the value thereof fixed by two impartial persons."

He was succeeded by Parson John Barnard in 1716, who continued till his death in 1770. He refused the presidency of Harvard in 1737, which was then accepted by Edward Holyoke of the Second Congregational Church—also of Marblehead. Meanwhile, St. Michael's (the oldest church building in New England) was built in 1714, cruciform in plan, and with frame and materials sent from England. It still retains its ancient reredos, with credo and decalogue, black with age,—although the original plan has been rather obscured by an addition added across one end. The Rev. David Mossom, its second rector, afterward removed to Virginia, where he married George Washington and Martha Custis.

Beside St. Michael's, the oldest church building now existing in Marblehead is the structure known as The Old North, on Washington Street, not far from the Old Town House, in the Square, and just beyond the Capt. Trevett House. This is the third edifice of the First Congregational Church, and dates from 1824. It has a granite façade, with an interesting tower or belfry, with a part of the sounding board from the second church pulpit, and an old fish weather-vane now on the tower, which was also taken from the second building, built in 1695. Of the original structure of the First Church, or Meeting House, there have been preserved several portions of the paneled fronts and doors of the old Oaken Pews, taken from this original building of 1648—which have never been painted, with the exception of the oval back of the pew number. While the mouldings and styles differ somewhat, yet they all exhibit a fine precision of workmanship,—and are perhaps the oldest bits of ecclesiastical architectural detail remaining in New England. The original pulpit of the third edifice, of rosewood, is in use in the present building.

It happens that we have another word picture of Marblehead; that given by Mr. Barnard, also when he arrived in the town, in November of 1715. He wrote, "There were two companies of poor, smoke dried, rude, ill clothed men without military discipline. There was not one proper carpenter, mason, tailor, nor butcher in the town nor any market worth naming. They had their houses built by country work-

especially so many early dwellings of three story height—as the early houses that have come down to this time still exhibit,—though it is to be remembered that it was during his ministry that the men were encouraged to take their own ships farther afield; and so secure to themselves the profits from their work, and bring back the much needed cash in exchange. It was from these ventures, finally, that the first merchant fortunes of the town were derived.

COL. WILLIAM R. LEE HOUSE—1745—WASHINGTON STREET, MARBLEHEAD

men, their clothes made out of town and supplied themselves with beef and pork from Boston, which drained the town of its money. Nor was there a foreign trading vessel belonging to the town. The people left the merchants of Boston, Salem, and Europe to carry away the gains by which means the town was always dismally poor and as rude, swearing, drunken and fighting a crew as they were poor."

It seems the more remarkable that from such rude surroundings should arise such fine dwellings—and

One of the most famous residents among the many who came from Marblehead, was the Col. John Glover, of the Fourteenth Continentals, of Revolutionary fame, who headed the "Amphibious Regiment" of Marbleheaders whose knowledge of the sea, and its tricks, made possibly two of the most famous exploits of Washington's army; and may have been instrumental in winning the war of Independence. These were, of course, the secret ferrying across the river from Long Island of the entire American army of 9000

Stair Hall
COL. WILLIAM R. LEE HOUSE—1745—MARBLEHEAD, MASSACHUSETTS

Staircase from First to Second Floor

Old Staircase, Rear of Second Floor

COL. WILLIAM R. LEE HOUSE—1745—WASHINGTON STREET, MARBLEHEAD, MASSACHUSETTS

Fireplace End — New Portion (c1780)

COL. WILLIAM R. LEE HOUSE — 1745 — WASHINGTON STREET, MARBLEHEAD, MASSACHUSETTS

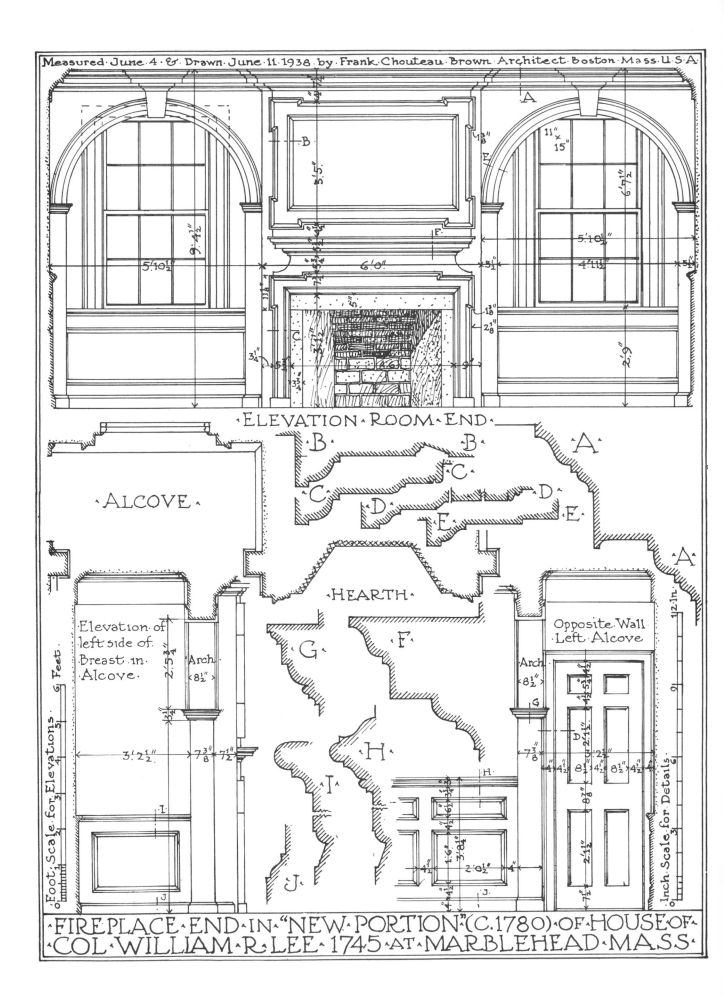

Measured June 4 & Drawn June 11 1938 by Frank Chouteau Brown Architect Boston Mass U.S.A.

· ELEVATION · ROOM · END ·

· ALCOVE ·

Elevation of
left side of
Breast in
Alcove.

· HEARTH ·

Opposite Wall
Left Alcove

· FIREPLACE · END · IN · "NEW · PORTION" · (C.1780) · OF · HOUSE · OF ·
· COL · WILLIAM · R · LEE · 1745 · AT · MARBLEHEAD · MASS ·

Drawing Room

Southeast Room — Second Floor
COL. WILLIAM R. LEE HOUSE — 1745 — MARBLEHEAD, MASSACHUSETTS

men, with horses, cannon and supplies, in one foggy
night, of thirteen hours; and the equally impossible
feat of crossing the Delaware in a winter storm on
Christmas Day and surprising the Hessians, secure in
their winter quarters at Trenton, outside Philadelphia.

John Glover was born in Salem, November 5, 1732.
With his three brothers, he came to Marblehead;
worked as shoemaker, fisherman, merchant, and
served in the militia, becoming a captain in 1773. He

group, would be Skipper Ireson of Whittier's poem
and Agnes Surriage, who in later years married Sir
Harry Frankland, whom she met when he—as Col-
lector of the Port of Boston—was often in Marblehead while superintending the construction of Fort
Sewall, at the entrance to the Harbor, in 1742.

Of the several old Lee family houses in Marblehead,
the Lee Mansion, was built in 1768 by Jeremiah
Lee, who died in 1775; and while the one perhaps best

Wall Paper in the Drawing Room
COL. WILLIAM R. LEE HOUSE—1745—MARBLEHEAD, MASSACHUSETTS

ended the War as a Brigadier-General, and served on
the court-martial that tried Maj. Andre. The front
of his house may be seen at the right of the illustration
at the bottom of page 100, (Volume III, Chapter 7).

Other famous Marbleheaders would include Com-
modore Samuel Tucker, Col. Azor Orne, Capt. John
Selman, Gov. Elbridge Gerry, Maj. John Pedrick,
Judge Joseph Story, Chief Justice Sewell, and Peter
Jayne. Two more, who belong almost to the legendary

known to visitors from being the home of the Marblehead Historical Society, and well filled with its treasures,—yet the home of Colonel William R. Lee, which
was earlier known as The House on the Hill for
thirty years or so before the Mansion was built, is one
of the most notable of the older landmarks of the
town. Placed looking south over the old Training
Field, it was originally a narrow two-room-to-the-
floor, three-story dwelling, with its end to the street;

and was certainly built as early as 1745, — and even may have been the house that was mentioned as being upon this site still twenty years earlier.

The house was built by Col. Lee's grandfather, Samuel Lee, and originally faced southwest, — while parts of the old stairway and hall, with the old front door, are still to be seen in their proper locations in the old building. But shortly after Jeremiah — who was the uncle of Col. Wm. R. Lee — built his Mansion

after the front portion was occupied; and has the curious newel and unusual baluster spacing that appears in the photographs. The new room at the southeast corner was given a new chimney and end treatment, with deep arched recesses, and the larger room across the hall was furnished, a few years later, with the gorgeous and unique oriental scenery paper known as The Pilgrimage of Omar showing a view of the Bosphorous and old Stamboul, which still retains all

Wall Paper in the Drawing Room
COL. WILLIAM R. LEE HOUSE — 1745 — MARBLEHEAD, MASSACHUSETTS

House further down the street, Col. Lee — who had formed the local artillery company — took off the easternmost room of the old house and built the "new front" facing southeast upon the street, and the old Training Field; raising the story heights, and taking the older carved balusters of the lower flight of the old stairway to use them over again in the new stairway and hall of the front part of the building. The "new stairway" was built about 1790, shortly

its striking colorfulness. It was probably made about 1800 — perhaps by Defour — and is not duplicated elsewhere in New England.

The Lee family originally came from Manchester, Massachusetts; and it was Justice Samuel L. Lee (1667–1754) who was also known as a builder and owner of numerous pieces of property, — as well as for being the father of thirteen children — who built the house now best known as the Colonel William Ray-

ST. MICHAEL'S CHURCH—1714—MARBLEHEAD, MASSACHUSETTS
Oldest Episcopal Church in New England

OLD NORTH CHURCH—1824—MARBLEHEAD, MASSACHUSETTS

mond Lee Dwelling. When the latter altered it, and added the new three story front sometime about 1780 to 1790, he greatly increased the story heights, making the new first floor 9'5" high where the old one was only 7'6", and so occasioning many interesting—and unexpected!—differences of level in going from one portion of the house to another, as well as requiring several short flights of stairs;—the last of which leads up to the level of the banquet room, which ran the entire width of the new front upon the upper story, between fireplaces of the same design placed at both ends.

The Lee Mansion below the Hill, and nearly across Bank Square from the "King" Hooper House, is one of the most-visited dwellings in New England. Its wide and spacious hallway (the first run of the staircase is over six feet wide, with mahogany balusters and trim—see Volume X, Chapter 12) with its old paper, which gray and white design is continued into the two front rooms upon the second floor, is justly famous. The banquet room here is upon the first floor, and the opposite room or parlor has a fine mantelpiece with pilasters, very much like one that was in the now vanished "Lindens" at Danvers. Even the kitchen has a magnificent paneled end, over a fireplace that is six feet long and four and a half feet high. This kitchen, by the way, opened at the rear, into an old passage that led to the slaves quarters and cookhouse,—a lower brick two-story building, still existing, at the right

of the main house, then providing shelter for the coach on the lower floor, and for the sleeping quarters of the slaves above it.

Not the least detail of interest in this fine old dwelling is the side stairway, that runs from the fine entrance on the northeast end, up to the third story, while the same baluster and post design continues from the middle of that floor up into the roof cupola. This stairway has an unusual, yet simple and practical, treatment of the wall dado, that has particular architectural interest. It should be noted that the main staircase does not continue above the second floor hall; the upper floor being reached only by this side stairway, or by means of a so-called secret stairway, off a closet beside the chimney between the bedrooms at the opposite end of the building.

These two principal front bedrooms are beautiful and spacious interiors, though the mantel pieces are much simpler than on the floor below, having only the large panels extending to the ceiling to mark their importance, compared to the pilasters framing the parlor fire-opening in the room at the right; and the fine and high relief carving, after the English manner, that ornaments the banquet room fireplace. In design and treatment the latter much resembles the carved oak mantel in the Bishop's Palace in Cambridge, Massachusetts,—although the work is here executed in pine, which is now grained, although originally believed to have been painted white.

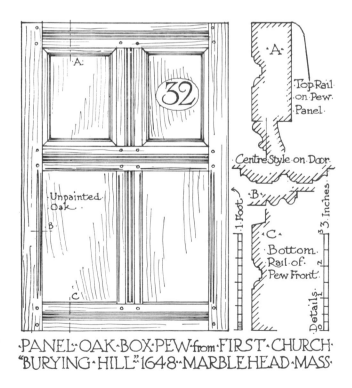

·PANEL·OAK·BOX·PEW·from·FIRST·CHURCH· "BURYING·HILL"·1648··MARBLEHEAD·MASS·

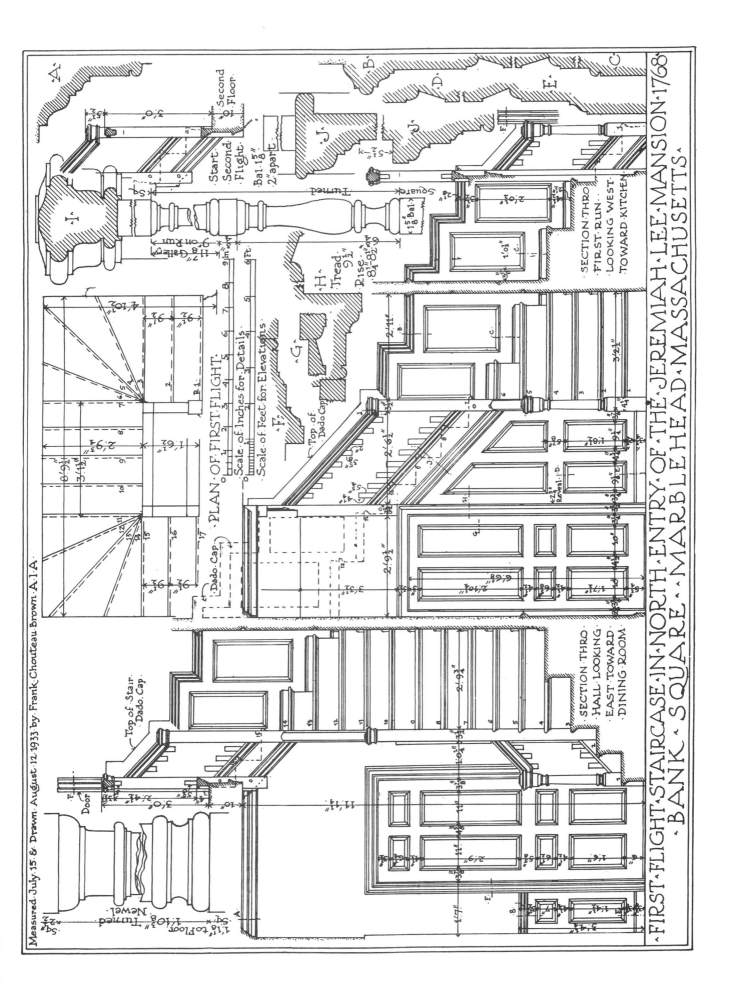

·FIRST·FLIGHT·STAIRCASE·IN·NORTH·ENTRY·OF·THE·JEREMIAH·LEE·MANSION·1768·
·BANK·SQUARE··MARBLEHEAD·MASSACHUSETTS·

Measured·July·15·& ·Drawn·August·12·1933·by·Frank·Chouteau·Brown·A·I·A·

·PLAN·OF·FIRST·FLIGHT·

Scale·of·Inches·for·Details

Scale·of·Feet·for·Elevations

·SECTION·THRO·
·FIRST·RUN·
·LOOKING·WEST·
·TOWARD·KITCHEN·

·SECTION·THRO·
·HALL·LOOKING·
·EAST·TOWARD·
·DINING·ROOM·

Detail of Façade
JEREMIAH LEE MANSION — 1768 — BANK SQUARE, MARBLEHEAD, MASSACHUSETTS

Old Marblehead, Part Three

Text by
Frank Chouteau Brown

Photographs by
Arthur C. Haskell

Originally published in 1938 as White Pine Monograph
Volume XXIV, Number 4

CAPT. ASA HOOPER HOUSE, 5 WASHINGTON STREET, MARBLEHEAD, MASSACHUSETTS

OLD MARBLEHEAD, MASSACHUSETTS
PART THREE

THE early growth of the town was not very rapid. By 1674 the town records had listed 114 householders; while in town meeting that same year it was voted that "all these fifteen or sixteen houses built in Marblehead before ye year 1660, shall be allowed one cowes common and a halfe." Most of the "Commons" set apart as public land owned in common by the community in the earlier settled townships of New England were intended either for grazing land, for the use of the cattle of the townspeople, or as a training field for the regular meetings of its "train band," the first colonial militia.

Besides its Training Field, the town early allotted "the Neck" for general use as "Cow Commons." The "Neck" was a rocky peninsula, almost entirely detached from the mainland, except at low tide, when a shallow sand bar from its westernmost end formed the inner limits of the large harbor. A slight obstruction across this natural causeway kept the cattle confined to the grazing area, even at low water. It was this same Neck—which was practically an island at high tide—that gave protection to the larger anchorage that is now known as the Harbor,—although in the first hundred years of its settlement, the fishermen and small vessels using the town facilities took advantage of the better protected Little Harbor, a small bay just back of the promontory crowned by Fort Sewall, at the very foot of Burying Hill, which was the site of the first settlement.

The importance of this harbor to the early settlement would be indicated by the several forts that were erected for its protection and defense at various times. Most important of these is Fort Sewall, built on the mainland side of the harbor entrance. This position was first fortified in very early times. During King Philip's War, which began in 1675 and continued for three years, this fort and its three large cannon were placed in order, and it has been continued and improved from time to time up nearly to the present day. The structure now to be seen dates from about 1742, when it was enlarged and reconstructed under Sir Harry Frankland. This position was garrisoned in three important wars and, although again somewhat rebuilt and remodeled in 1864, it still retains the older magazine, along with several old gun emplacements and other features.

Another old fort, known as Fort Washington, was constructed and in use during the Revolution and the War of 1812, on the high rocky bluff overlooking Orne Street, from near the Old Burying Hill, although, along with an embankment that at one time dominated the causeway, at the southern end of the main harbor, it has long since disappeared. One other earthwork fortification could, until within the last dozen years, be plainly traced at Naugus Head—the tip of the Cape nearest Salem Harbor. The dirt roadway around that headland that served a group of summer cottages cut right through the embankment in two places, and its main outlines were still easily traced, despite the location of some of the houses across and upon its outer slopes.

Along with this group might be mentioned the old Powder House, a fine example of the town magazine of the time, that was built by vote of the town, in 1755, at the outbreak of the French and Indian War, and continued in use through the Revolution and the War of 1812. It is a handsome example of brickwork, laid in Flemish bond, circular in plan and with a brick-domed top, covered by its ogee shingled roof, located on what used to be known as the Ferry Road. It is about the earliest and best example of a building of this type remaining within the Commonwealth; although the Gun House, built to house the artillery of the local regiment during the War of 1812, is probably more unique. In its simplicity this unusual building might almost suggest a post-Colonial precedent for the modern garage, if to be built of brick! The principal walls are again laid in an early bond.

This records an unusual number of public buildings, of both age and historic association, still preserved in one small township,—except that no specific mention has yet been made of the old Town House (illus-

ROBIE HOUSE—1729—7 PEARL STREET, MARBLEHEAD, MASSACHUSETTS

trated in Vol. III, Chap. 7), which was built in 1727 exclusively for that purpose and continued in use until 1877, when Abbot Hall, an ugly brick structure of Victorian type, was built on the old Training Field and given to the townspeople for a meeting place. The Old Town House formerly had a Market under it on the ground floor level—as was so commonly the case in many sections of old England—which also explains its high basement, now occupied by the local constabulary, to which it gives dignified shelter.

a successful economic solution for his pastorate from those conditions amongst which he had found them than upon his eminence as a spiritual leader. For Marblehead—in common with most other smaller townships—was then desperately contending for its prosperity and future livelihood against capitalistic control, in the first instance imposed by its English sponsors, but later furthered both by the governmental and merchandising functions common to the period. So long as the residents of this little fishing

AZOR ORNE HOUSE, ORNE STREET, MARBLEHEAD, MASSACHUSETTS

If we glance back over the early records of the colonies, it will be realized that there must have been more than a merely spiritual reason for all the early settlement groups to have so continually evolved about their preacher's leadership. He must have possessed temporal as well as spiritual power to have been able to lead his flock successfully into this new world wilderness, and bring them to a permanent fruition. And so it would seem that the high repute attained by Parson John Barnard in this community was based rather upon his business acumen in finding

community were content to remain an adjunct to the larger and more prosperous trading port of nearby Salem; so long as they were content to endure the privations inherent in the fisherman's calling, and allow the merchants of Salem to carry their product to the larger cities where it was most in demand, they must also expect them to obtain the major part of the profits. And the more especially when they were accustomed to accept, locally, other merchandise in exchange for their fish; while these middlemen merchants took to themselves not only the ample benefits

Room with Paneled End

Room with Paneled End
ORNE HOUSE, ORNE STREET, MARBLEHEAD, MASSACHUSETTS

of coined currency payments for the fish, but also exacted metal money payment for the costs of its carriage to market!

And it was this problem that Parson Barnard solved by persuading the Marbleheaders to convey their own fish to market, and so themselves profit both from the savings made in its transport and the currency payments. It was shortly after this that the town entered upon its new prosperity and period of more pretentious building. And, at once, some of the new three

the walls of the two-storied main hall, and the two principal rooms upon the second floor. Obviously, all of the panels originally must have been painted to fit the spaces between doors and window trim, and extending from dado cap to cornice facia.

The Jeremiah Lee Mansion is, perhaps, almost the best New England example of that type of Colonial architecture that might be most correctly termed Georgian,—a word much misused! In old England it usually refers to a structure of similar design, but

Fireplace and Paneling, Second Floor
JEREMIAH LEE MANSION—1768—MARBLEHEAD, MASSACHUSETTS

story dwellings—including probably the Robie House, of brick, built about 1729—began to demonstrate this new influx of wealth. And from then on, as in the other houses already illustrated, did the architecture of the town express the change in its manners of living, culminating finally in the Lee Mansion, of 1768.

Some further evidence of its dignified detail, furnishing, and decoration appears on these pages, including particularly the fine mantels, and the unusual painted wall coverings executed in gray monotone and white, in the classical fashion of the time, that extend over

generally built of either brick or stone. In America, brick was also used generally for dwellings of this kind in the South, but in the New England colonies—where wood was always the favored material—it was sometimes, as in this present instance, employed so as to suggest, or rather to simulate, the formal stone coursing of England—as in the regions around Bath—for a dwelling of this pretentious kind.

So the use of wooden boards, with both horizontal and perpendicular grooves, disposed to suggest the jointing of a masonry wall, was not an uncommon

Banquet Room

JEREMIAH LEE MANSION—1768—BANK SQUARE, MARBLEHEAD, MASSACHUSETTS

Fireplace and Paneling, Second Floor Family Living Room

JEREMIAH LEE MANSION—1768—BANK SQUARE, MARBLEHEAD, MASSACHUSETTS

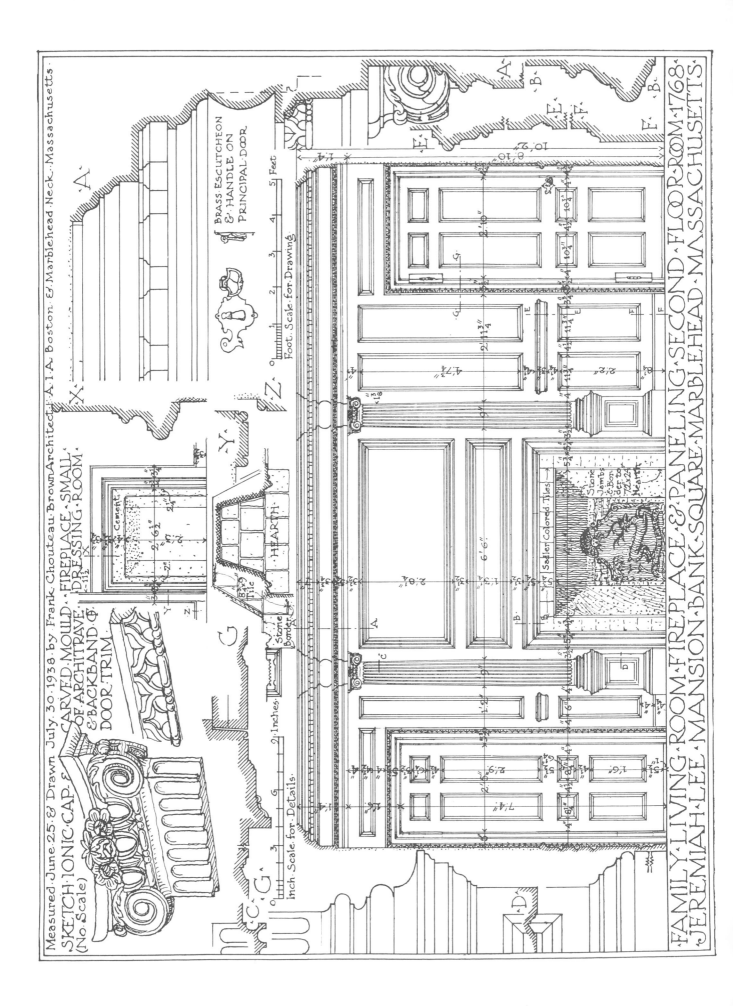

Dining Room Mantel

Drawing Room Mantel

JEREMIAH LEE MANSION — 1768 — BANK SQUARE, MARBLEHEAD, MASSACHUSETTS

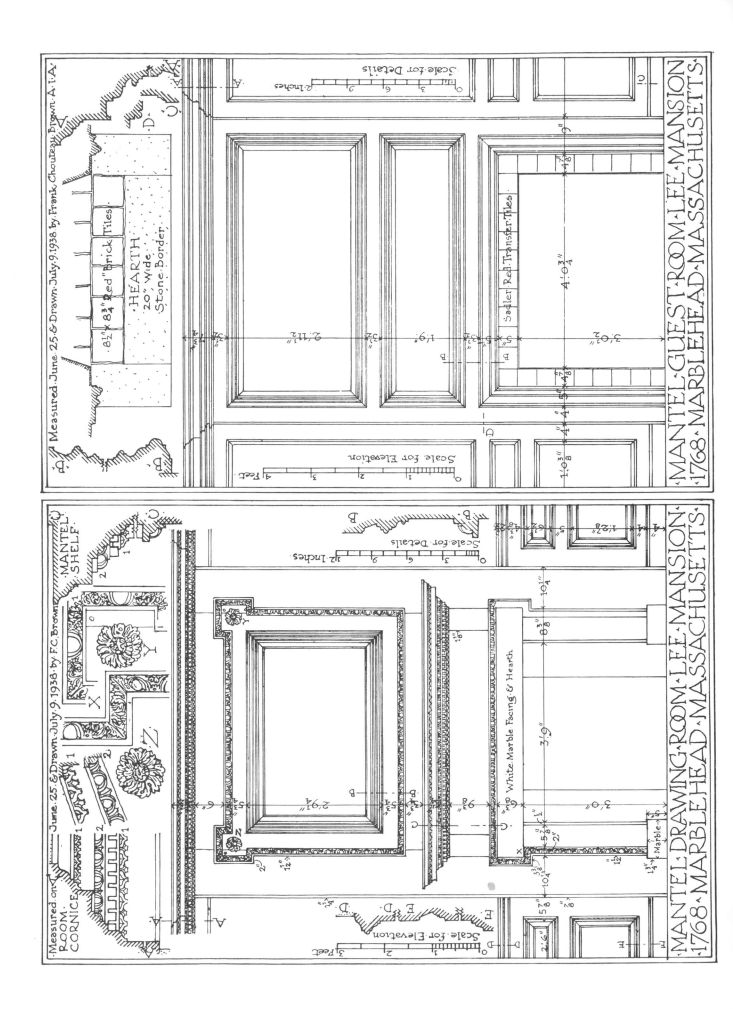

·MANTEL·GUEST·ROOM·LEE·MANSION·
·1768·MARBLEHEAD·MASSACHUSETTS·

·MANTEL·DRAWING·ROOM·LEE·MANSION·
·1768·MARBLEHEAD·MASSACHUSETTS·

Corner of Banquet Room

Kitchen

JEREMIAH LEE MANSION — 1768 — BANK SQUARE, MARBLEHEAD, MASSACHUSETTS

LOWER WASHINGTON STREET, LOOKING NORTH

GUN HOUSE

GLIMPSES OF OLD BUILDINGS WHICH ABOUND IN MARBLEHEAD, MASSACHUSETTS

treatment for important dwellings in towns along the coast. In some cases it was employed upon the front alone. In other instances it was used upon the front and two ends; and sometimes—although more rarely —on all four sides of the structure. In Marblehead, both the Lee houses—as well as the "King" Hooper House—have shown this use of wood as an outer wall covering. So, too, did the "Lindens," formerly in Danvers; and it is also occasionally found on dwellings in Salem, Hingham, Newburyport, Portsmouth, Portland, Providence, and other cities and towns in New England. It is an even more common treatment to find wooden quoins used on the corners of old Colonial wooden buildings in place of the simpler upright corner board.

Another feature employed in common by the two Lee Houses, is the cupola on the center of the roof ridge,—that, in the more dignified and formally designed coast dwelling, sometimes supplants the simpler "Captain's Walk," that was built over the roofs of many old houses along the coast, at the old harbors of the mainland and, especially, in great numbers, in such a seafaring island port as Nantucket. Their chief reason for being was to give the occupants of these houses easy access to the roof to overlook and keep track of the shipping in the harbor and the boats that entered and left its anchorage on their many voyages from the port.

Both Jeremiah Lee and Col. Azor Orne were elected to the Continental Congress, as well as being members of the province "Committee of Safety and Supplies," and the two, along with their fellow-townsman, Elbridge Gerry (afterwards vice-president of the United States), were very nearly surprised at Cambridge by the British soldiers, on the night of April 18, 1775, when they had remained in the Black Horse Tavern after a later meeting of the province committee, escaping at the very last moment, with only a few clothes, —of the result of which exposure Mr. Lee died just three weeks later.

The Azor Orne House is another Marblehead example of the three-story town house—although, rather unusually, with gable ends; and a late doorway—of which, however, the rear view shown here is more locally characteristic; indicating, as it does, the way the houses in that town are sometimes located against the base of the rocky bluffs that often crowd upon and overlook their narrow backyards. This dwelling is situated on the street of the same name, off the turn at the end of Washington Street into Franklin, facing out toward the harbor. The home of Parson Barnard is on Franklin Street, just around the corner; a large

gambrel roof dwelling, enshrouded in fine old trees, of nice proportions, but with little authentic detail remaining from its many changes and repairs.

Inside its later Greek doorway, the Orne House has a fine stairway of the period of about 1770, with fireplaces and cornices quite similar to those of the simpler types to be found in the Lee Mansion; along with the rooms with simple paneled end, of which two examples are shown herewith.

But, after all, the distinctive charm of Marblehead does not reside in its more pretentious dwellings, handsome and much visited as they are; but rather in the more informal and picturesque groupings of old weatherworn sided structures, placed at all possible angles to the street, and to their neighbors, in which certain sections of the old town still abound. While, to a lesser extent, at Newcastle and upon some portions of the old River Road along the Merrimac in Amesbury, and at one or two sections of Portsmouth, and a few bits around the harbor at Gloucester, a few similar glimpses may now be seen—and, to an even greater extent, they will probably continue and be preserved on the island at Nantucket—certainly nowhere else so near to Boston may so much of the charm of an old informally developed fishing port still be seen by the hurried visitor.

Repairs and rebuildings by natives and summer visitors; repainting, clapboarding, and new wall-shinglings by the stiff-necked "Headers"; with clumsy-carpentered replacements, entirely lacking the old character that has made this town so attractive to visitors in the past, still goes doggedly on, year after year,—until now there remain only a few of the many picturesque groupings that formerly abounded on every side. Such glimpses as of the North Church tower from Back Street (page 123, Vol. III, Chap. 8); the bit on Lower Washington Street (page 140); or the view nearly behind that place, across the back yards off Pearl Street (page 142); the bit to be seen on the S-shaped zig-zag down the hill from Lee Street onto Front (page 142)—although now much less interesting than before the old fish-warehouse was "slicked up" a few years ago!—or, finally, and most characteristically, the old lobsterman's shack surrounded by lobster pots and dories, down near the Little Harbor beach, are fast disappearing, along with other well-remembered vistas—such as the old Spite House before it was painted a few years ago. They now linger in the memories of a few older inhabitants, a fewer number of old visitors,—and where they have been recorded for posterity, as vanishing records from the nation's picturesque and "functional" past, as upon these pages—and others in this series—will continue to show!

ACROSS THE BACK YARDS OFF PEARL STREET

HEAD OF FRONT STREET

TWO OF THE MANY PICTURESQUE GROUPINGS OF BUILDINGS IN MARBLEHEAD, MASSACHUSETTS

Cape Ann Cottages

Text by
Daniel O. Brewster

Photographs by
Arthur C. Haskell

Originally published in 1933 as White Pine Monograph
Volume XIX, Number 6

OLD TARR HOMESTEAD, 6 SOUTH STREET, ROCKPORT, MASSACHUSETTS

THE COTTAGES OF CAPE ANN

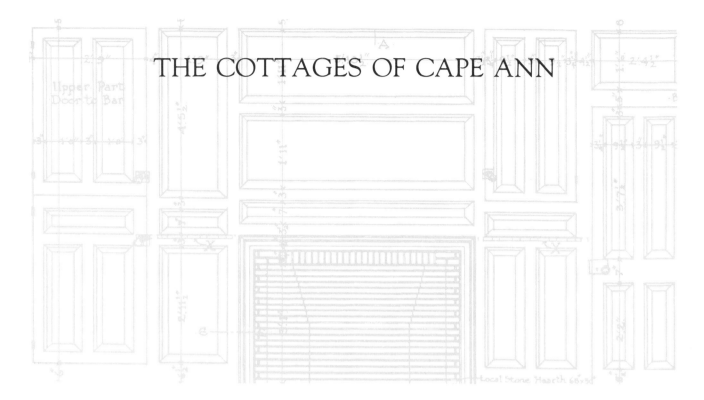

THE early Colonial cottage, wherever it may still be found unspoiled by later additions and changes, possesses a charm and attraction that is not always conveyed by its larger and more formal dwelling associate. Usually of only one story, or a story and a half in height, it generally contains only two to three rooms upon the first floor, and its plan is of the simplest — an entrance near one end, a room along what remains of the front, and the rear space divided into two rooms in width.

When the plan is of less depth than that required for two rooms, the entrance may be nearer the middle of the front, and a room at either side; or, if the door and stairs remain near one end, there may be an ell extended at one side, instead of at the rear, as is more likely to be the case with a larger type of plan. And frequently these ells are either built on at later dates, or even a shed moved up against the cottage and connected with it — usually performing the function of a service or kitchen addition.

The upper story may be left unfinished, or divided into a couple of rooms — rarely more, as the dormers now found in the sloping roofs are almost invariably of a date subsequent to the original construction. The chimney — overlarge for its diminutive plan — was generally placed back of the hall and stairway, as was the custom with the larger houses of the period. In that location it could serve the two larger rooms, of which one was the kitchen — or combined kitchen and living room — and the other a sleeping room off the kitchen, found in so many of the larger dwellings of that time.

The earliest type will be shown in the original Riggs House (Vol. III, Chap. 14), a three-room structure of squared logs with a pitch roof. And the same dwelling shows, in its later addition, the gambrel-roof type that came into local fashion just about the end of the seventeenth century, and continued to be the almost invariable arrangement until well past the middle of the eighteenth. Between about 1690 and 1760, almost all the smaller dwellings on the Cape were of either the steep or flat gambrel design; by far the larger number being of the comfortable squat outline seen in so many of these accompanying illustrations.

This early squat gambrel roof gradually became steeper and sharper in pitch, until it was succeeded by a flatter single-slope pitched roof near the end of the eighteenth century, which, with its smaller chimney, soon came to mark the cottage of the early nineteenth. Perhaps the dormers covered by a simple extension of the upper roof slope may have been the earlier type — though even they are seldom to be found occurring in the original construction of the Cape cottage. They were probably soon succeeded by the gable-fronted dormer treatment, of which the most authentic and earliest example to be seen in this group of illustrations is the dormer on the "Cottage at the Head of the Cove" in Annisquam.

And so, too, the very modesty of these early cottage dwellings makes it difficult to find many whose early history and exact date of construction are known. Usually one is dependent upon some family legend, or the stories carried down to some existing "early inhabitant" by his elders, for a clue to the early ownership or records of these simple dwellings.

Cape Ann—named by Prince Charles after his mother, Anne of Denmark, wife of James I—extends about eight miles into the Atlantic, separating Massachusetts and Ipswich Bays, and has an area of about forty-three square miles. The entire coast line is very irregular, and starting at "The Cut"—a short canal cut at an early date to connect the tip of Squam River with Gloucester Harbor—its margin is occupied by a continuous settlement, the principal sections of which are known by many descriptive local names, such as, Riverdale, Annisquam, Bay View, Lanesville, Folly Cove, Pigeon Cove, Sandy Bay (now Rockport), Straitsmouth, Land's End, Long Beach, Bass Rocks, East Gloucester, and the Harbor. On the interior are the Farms and the legendary ruins of Dogtown Common, while a considerable area of land upon the mainland is also known as West Gloucester, extending toward Essex and Ipswich and along the Magnolia Shore.

About 1700, or soon thereafter, one Joshua Norwood came and settled on Gully Point, Straitsmouth, near Land's End, where he built a log cabin, which was afterwards removed to Dock Square, where it now stands at one side of Atlantic Avenue; with the Hannah Jumper House upon the other, the two being among the oldest cottages in Rockport. The rough log construction of the former may still be seen inside.

Nearby, the gambrel-roofed cottage of Francis ("Red Cap") Norwood still overlooks the harbor from its old location back from the more modern Atlantic Avenue. It was built about 1720, and its large central chimney contains the two largest fireplaces in the town. From Dock Square, the main road to Land's End is first known as Mt. Pleasant, then as South Street, and this section is usually called Cove Hill, and leads to the South End. Number Six South Street, built well before 1750, probably about 1725, is a typical gambrel-roof cottage, which has been unusually well cared for and preserved. While just across Prospect Street is another old cottage, originally belonging either to an early Poole or another Tarr family offshoot, which has been recently restored. Farther along South Street is a veritable *congerie* of Smith, Poole, and Tarr family dwellings, all dating from about 1750 to 1775.

Most of the small dwellings that once crowded the lanes and streets of Gloucester and Rockport have been replaced by the newer buildings and "improvements" called for by the prosperity and growing business of these centers, but a few still remain tucked away

OLD WOODBURY HOUSE—c1665–1670—ANNISQUAM, MASSACHUSETTS
Now Kitchen Ell Back of Main House

JOSHUA NORWOOD'S CABIN, ROCKPORT, MASSACHUSETTS
Known as the Oldest House in Rockport

in the older streets and back corners of the towns, where business has not yet come to disturb them.

As was so often the case, these little cottages were originally built facing to the south, at a time when there were no established streets—and even the main travelled roads were an informal and movable element in the community, the houses being most usually approached across fields or woodlands by means of a footpath. It has been the fate of many of these original homesteads to be later turned into the kitchen or service portions of larger houses, later built to front the streets—as in the old Woodbury Cottage at Annisquam (page 146). Again and again, their compactness has made it easy for their owners to remove themselves, with bag and baggage, and almost bearing their "cot" upon their backs, to a new and more convenient situation. This is a pilgrimage that has happened to more than a few of the houses illustrated in this present group.

Most frequently—where still upon their original foundations—they now stand at all angles to later-day streets, which—particularly upon the Cape—wind their way about, while avoiding the sturdy ledge outcroppings and irregular boulder-droppings left by the

terminal moraine that scarred and grooved the contours of the township. Latter-day dwellings may front primly upon street and square; and often jostle the corners of their older associates in the doing o't; but the little dwellings of the earlier generations remain undisturbed and placid among them, secure in their possession of that same vague but unescapable "it," that is so woefully lacking in the construction of later generations, particularly the houses—of whatever size—built from about 1830, or during this last century "of progress."

In fact, one rather suspects that some part of their compositional charm may come from this very informality of relation to the street lines before them; forcing that glimpse of the front at an angle that shows the spectator also a considerable part of the house-end gable—this being rather an advantage than a disadvantage in the general appearance and appeal made by these unpretentious dwellings.

But so many have been irretrievably spoiled by ill-advised and crudely undertaken alterations and additions! For every one photographed, at least a dozen have been passed by because of the unfeeling treatment, rather than the neglect, to which they have been

COTTAGE BACK OF OLD BURYING GROUND—1750—ROCKPORT, MASSACHUSETTS

OLD COTTAGE BACK FROM ROAD—1720—ANNISQUAM, MASSACHUSETTS

OLD COTTAGES BESIDE ROAD TO EAST GLOUCESTER, MASSACHUSETTS

COTTAGE ON WALNUT STREET — c1760 — ANNISQUAM, MASSACHUSETTS

OLD TARR HOMESTEAD, 6 SOUTH STREET, ROCKPORT, CAPE ANN, MASSACHUSETTS

OLD COTTAGE AT HEAD OF THE COVE — c1725 — ANNISQUAM, CAPE ANN, MASSACHUSETTS

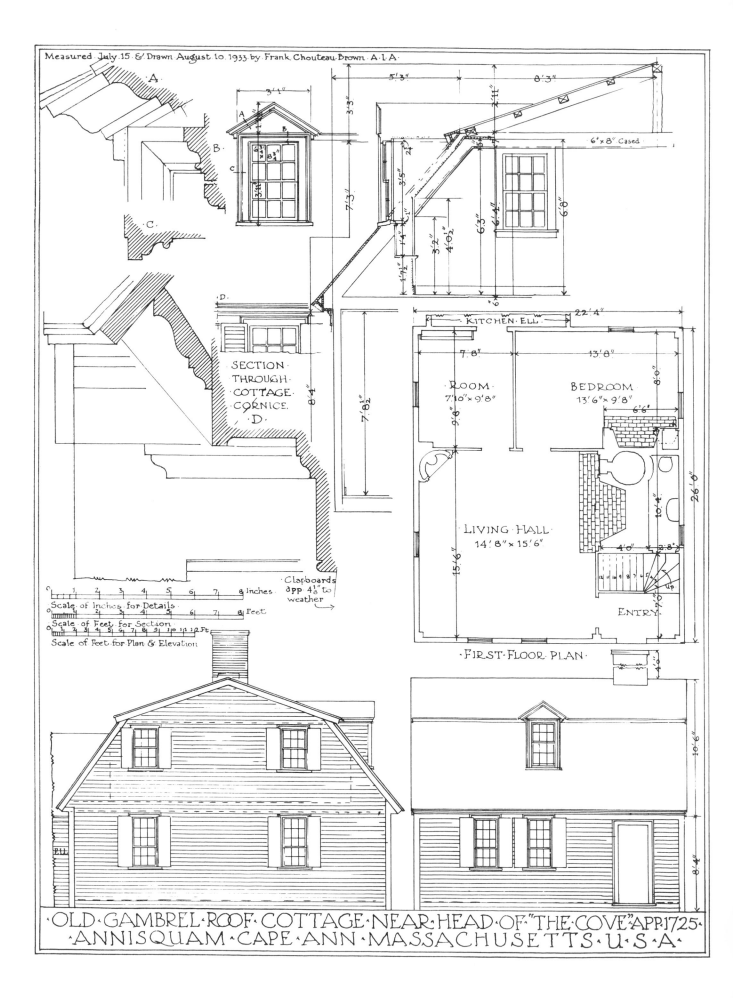

Measured July 15 & Drawn August 10, 1933 by Frank Chouteau Brown A.I.A.

A

B

C

A
B
C

D

SECTION
THROUGH
COTTAGE
CORNICE
· D ·

6" x 8" Cased

Clapboards
app 4½" to
weather

Scale of Inches for Details
Scale of Feet for Section
Scale of Feet for Plan & Elevation

Inches

Feet

KITCHEN ELL

22'4"

ROOM
7'10" x 9'8"

BEDROOM
13'6" x 9'8"

LIVING HALL
14'8" x 15'6"

ENTRY

· FIRST · FLOOR · PLAN ·

·OLD·GAMBREL·ROOF·COTTAGE·NEAR·HEAD·OF·"THE·COVE"·APP·1725·
·ANNISQUAM·CAPE·ANN·MASSACHUSETTS·U·S·A·

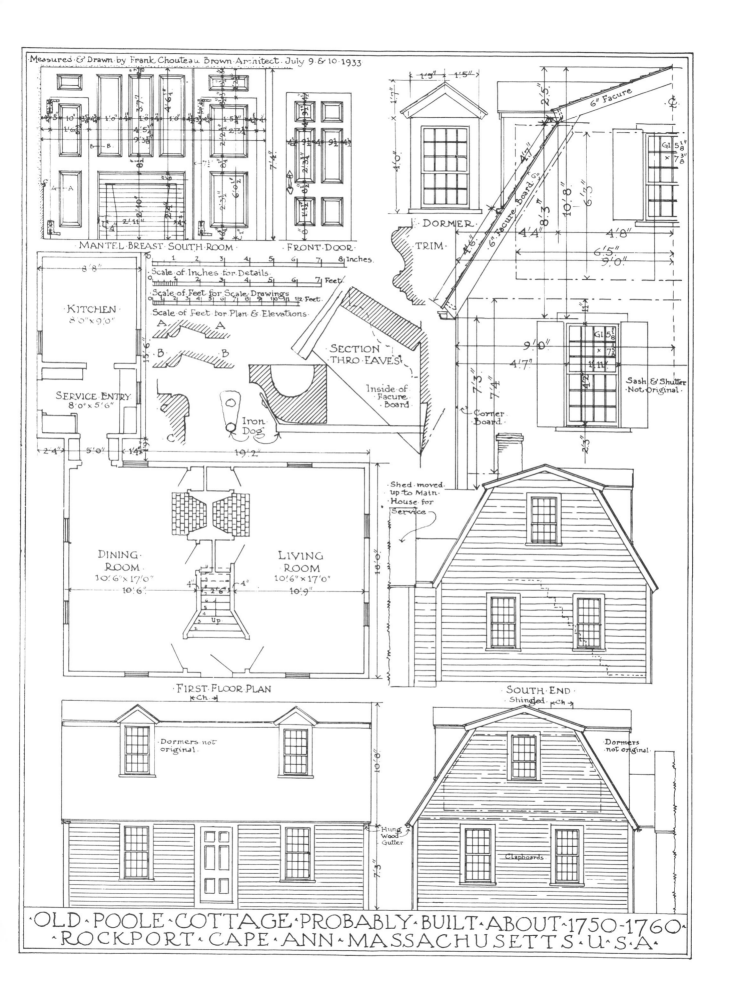

Measured & Drawn by Frank Chouteau Brown Architect July 9 & 10 1933

MANTEL BREAST SOUTH ROOM

FRONT DOOR

DORMER TRIM

KITCHEN
8'0" x 9'0"

SERVICE ENTRY
8'0" x 5'6"

Scale of Inches for Details.
Scale of Feet for Scale Drawings
Scale of Feet for Plan & Elevations

SECTION THRO EAVES

Inside of Facure Board

Iron Dog

6" Facure

6" Facure Board

Gl 5⅛" x 7⅞"

Sash & Shutter Not Original.

Corner Board

DINING ROOM
10'6" x 17'0"
10'6"

LIVING ROOM
10'6" x 17'0"
10'9"

Up

FIRST FLOOR PLAN

Shed moved up to Main House for Service

SOUTH END
Shingled

Hung Wood Gutter

Dormers not original.

Dormers not original.

Clapboards

OLD·POOLE·COTTAGE·PROBABLY·BUILT·ABOUT·1750-1760·
ROCKPORT·CAPE·ANN·MASSACHUSETTS·U·S·A·

forcibly subjected! Mere neglect usually but adds illusion to the element of the picturesque. But the country carpenter—even possibly the city architect of general practice—may not possess that delicate sensibility that is necessary to take over these simple little survivors of an early age, and continue their charm and beauty, in a little enlarged and perhaps more fully dormered —and, possibly, also plumbered!—version.

Even some among the cottages illustrated here may be remembered by a fortunate few "early inhabitants" in a previous and more charming state than that to which they have now attained—especially where they are now to be seen in a snugly washed and starched Sunday best. To many their older, more ordinary, workaday appearance, may have been preferable! One can understand the Puritan's aversion to paint, as one recalls their vanished picturesqueness. No "paint up" and "clean up" campaigns in those days, we may be assured. And nowadays we have to suffer from our inordinate belief in neatness, cleanness, sanitation and efficiency, being the very be-all and end-all desired of our day and generation!

OLD POOLE (CAPT. TARR) COTTAGE—1750–1760—ROCKPORT, MASSACHUSETTS

LANE HOMESTEAD — c1825 — ANNISQUAM, MASSACHUSETTS

CAPT. WOODBURY HOUSE, FOLLY COVE, CAPE ANN, MASSACHUSETTS

FRANCIS ("RED CAP") NORWOOD HOUSE—1700-1720—OVERLOOKING HARBOR, ROCKPORT, MASSACHUSETTS

GAMAGE HOUSE — c1725 — HIGH STREET, ROCKPORT, CAPE ANN, MASSACHUSETTS

LANGFORD HOMESTEAD — c1760 — LANESVILLE, MASSACHUSETTS

CLARK COTTAGE — c1750 — 8 BEACON STREET, GLOUCESTER, MASSACHUSETTS

BUTMAN HOUSE—1760—ROCKPORT, MASSACHUSETTS

GAMBREL END COTTAGE WITH "JUTBY", MAIN STREET, PIGEON COVE, MASSACHUSETTS

Cape Ann Cottage Interiors

Text by
M. S. Franklin

Photographs by
Arthur C. Haskell

Originally published in 1933 as White Pine Monograph
Volume XX, Number 1

Detail of Living Room-Kitchen
OLD COTTAGE AT HEAD OF THE COVE, ANNISQUAM, MASSACHUSETTS

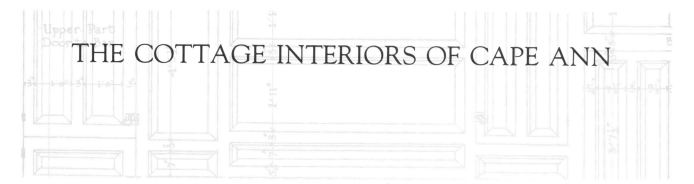

THE COTTAGE INTERIORS OF CAPE ANN

AFTER having recognized all those elements that go to make up the picturesqueness and informality of appeal possessed by the simpler types of early dwellings that we usually recall by the use of the term "cottage"; one must as well realize that these same factors may be extended within doors to help render these same dwellings as reposeful and satisfying to their occupants as they appear to the casual visitor or passerby from without. Many of the elements remain the same. Always is there evident simplicity and informality; the lack of pretense or any attempt at artifice or intentional assumption of superiority. Instead they radiate an atmosphere of homeliness; of everyday comfort and use; of simplicity and friendliness. All this becomes evident from the first glance at the low and inviting entrance; the low-lying roof, set close over the first floor windows; the windows themselves, broken up into many small and beautifully proportioned panes widened by their open shutters of heavy blinds and narrow intervening wall spaces. The first floor itself is set close down upon the ground. Even if the plan is more spacious than at first seems possible, the depth of the house is not felt because of the flattened gambrel that is so consistent and frequent a part of their design; and has so much to do with making them appear intimate and hospitable.

Deriving, as so many of them do, from an early period—when the conventions of village life were simple and its conveniences slight, they reflect upon their exterior the low ceiling heights and close-grouped windows that in turn do so much to make their small —yet usually ample—interiors seem cosy and homelike; shutting out the outdoors sufficiently, while making its human occupants comfortable beside the warm hearth and wide fireplace that so dominates the principal living room.

The very spacing of the windows themselves— usually set farther away from the house corners upon the exterior than would at first seem pleasing or necessary—upon the interior show that this suggestion of clustering, not only gives better wall space backing for the customary furniture of the family, but also tends to increase the atmosphere of comfort and seclusion.

And that small, almost minuteness of, scale! A scale that takes cognizance of the necessities of the human form—and but little more. Doors of a bare six feet of needed height! (Often one wonders what became of the large and gangling Yankee of tradition —and, for that matter—of established fact and record, as well!) Windows whose tops but barely permit the standing human visage to peer forth without an humbling of the body—if not the spirit!—and leave no room whatever for the continually lowered and hiding shades of but a few generations ago.

Yet the mouldings are never small and petty, as is so frequently the case in modern work. Their sections are satisfyingly full bodied, and restfully ample, sturdy and mannish in feel. They are never nervous or disturbing; and especially when they have been allowed to remain without paint, toned only by exposure to the light, and warmed by the patina of time and use, they possess such individuality as warms the owner's life and gives rest to his soul.

Certainly, no one can visit many of these dwellings, however cursorily, without being forced to accept the persisting legend that they must have been built and occupied in large part by the same owners and builders as worked upon the sailing vessels of the time. They still reflect the compactness and details of the pinks and pinnaces, the sloops and schooners, brigs and barks, that were then being built and outfitted along the shores of these landlocked coves and harbors.

In proof of this conclusion, one has merely to regard the careful workmanship and expert joining to be found in the paneling and dado sections, the doors and mantels, of any of these older cottage dwellings. Who but an owner-carpenter, delighting in the problems of his trade and the use of his hands during long winter days and evenings, would work out so lovingly the charming mouldings and ornaments of these interior details, the soft flowing outlines of the cupboard standards, the handworked—almost to say "hand carved" and enriched—moldings along mantelshelf and cupboard cornice? Who else would think out such minor refinements and conveniences as the tran-

Stair Well
COTTAGE AT HEAD OF THE COVE,
ANNISQUAM, MASSACHUSETTS

supplied by a piece of rope or cable, reeved through a ring at top and bottom of a steep stair flight, and held in place by some elaborately knotted device worked out upon the separated strands of the rope's ends. This sort of handrail is sometimes locally found, in conjunction with a steeply rising flight of steps such as could only have been inspired originally by some compact and shipshape schooner's cabin scuttle.

Sometimes the staircases pile steeply upward, in one short steep run, from entrance floor to dormered rooms above; sometimes they make the single winding turn of the old Tarr Homestead, against the large buttressed chimney of the early century. If so, the earlier examples may often be as simple as this instance; where the only change has been the insertion of a single wide board to fill in the space between the running rails that were originally open; and are also often found with added later balusters as has been done in the Francis Norwood House.

The Tarr Homestead has been far less disturbed than most of its sister dwellings, and so still provides the several charming views that go to illustrate some of the several elements claimed in these accompanying words, to make these cottages distinctive over their

som panel over the kitchen-living room door in the Annisquam Cottage, for instance—to give added ventilation and circulation in both hot summer days and nights, or in the long cold winters.

And, again, the heavy latticing of the second-story stair well guards—with irregularly cut and fitted cross pieces, set at no uniform or established degree of slope; but yet proportioned with exceptional feeling for the scale of its surroundings and a nice adaptation to place.

In this same house may be found, in the upper story, an end paneled into the gambrel slope of the roof; while the Francis Norwood Cottage in Rockport provides two similar second-story paneled ends, of which a few other examples also still exist about the neighborhood—all evidently dating well back into an early and primitive Cape period previous to 1750. And in these unpretentious types of cottage building, again, only a notable pride of craftsmanship along with an owner's innate interest—combined with a certain proportion of leisure time—would seem to warrant such unusual expenditures of labor, time, thought and pains upon comparatively unimportant rooms in these unpretentious and modest homes.

Often the marine customs of their builders and inhabitants is evidenced by the informal stair guidance

Entry
COTTAGE AT HEAD OF THE COVE,
ANNISQUAM, MASSACHUSETTS

Mantel and Paneled End of Living Room

COTTAGE AT HEAD OF THE COVE—1700–1725—ANNISQUAM, CAPE ANN, MASSACHUSETTS

Living Room
COTTAGE AT HEAD OF THE COVE—1700–1725—ANNISQUAM, MASSACHUSETTS

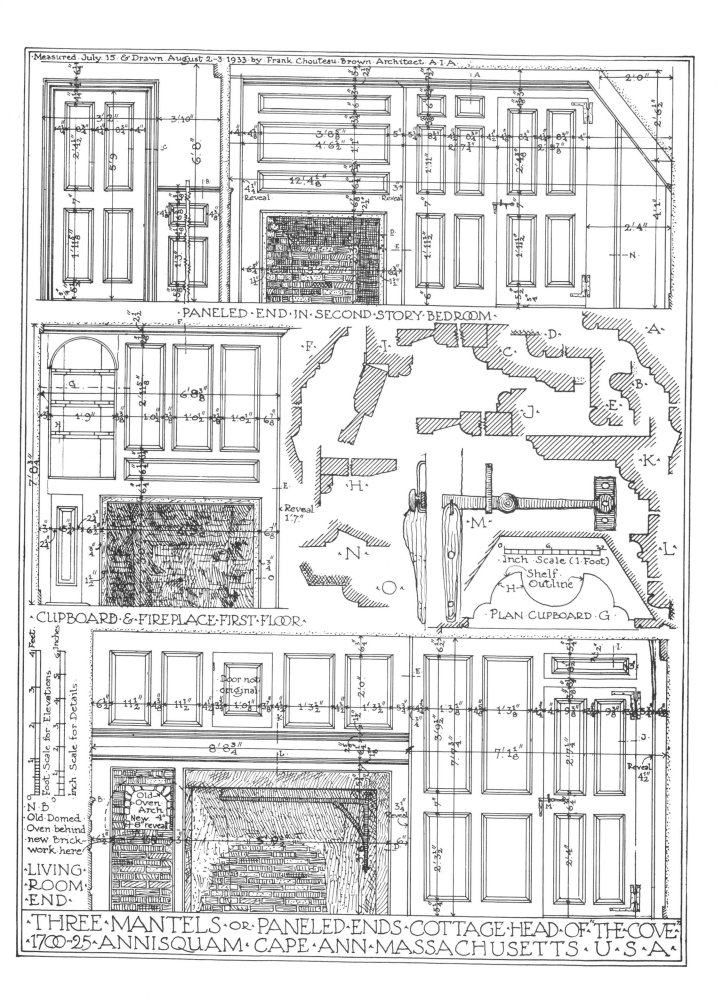

Measured July 15 & Drawn August 2-3 1933 by Frank Chouteau Brown Architect A·I·A·

·PANELED·END·IN·SECOND·STORY·BEDROOM·

·CUPBOARD·&·FIREPLACE·FIRST·FLOOR·

Inch Scale (1 Foot)

Shelf Outline

·PLAN·CUPBOARD·G·

Door not original

N·B·
Old·Domed·Oven·behind new brick-work·here·

·LIVING·ROOM·END·

Old Oven Arch New 4" reveal

·THREE·MANTELS·OR·PANELED·ENDS·COTTAGE·HEAD·OF·"THE·COVE"·
·1700-25·ANNISQUAM·CAPE·ANN·MASSACHUSETTS·U·S·A·

Second Story Bedroom

Paneled End in Second Story Bedroom
COTTAGE AT HEAD OF THE COVE —1700-1725— ANNISQUAM, MASSACHUSETTS

Cupboard and Fireplace — First Floor
COTTAGE AT HEAD OF THE COVE — 1700-1725 — ANNISQUAM, MASSACHUSETTS

Fireplace and Mantel in Living Hall
OLD TARR HOMESTEAD — 1750 — ROCKPORT, CAPE ANN, MASSACHUSETTS

Fireplace in Dining Room (Old Kitchen)
OLD TARR HOMESTEAD — 1750 — ROCKPORT, CAPE ANN, MASSACHUSETTS

Stairway
FRANCIS NORWOOD HOUSE,
ROCKPORT, MASSACHUSETTS

more formal brethren.

The interiors of both this Tarr Homestead and the Annisquam Cottage, however, are rarely interesting from the success with which the owners have found and arranged fittings consistent with the early period and use of these homes.

In Annisquam, the Cottage at the Head of the Cove (and while there are several "coves" in Annisquam, there is only one "THE Cove"!) gains in atmosphere by still displaying the tone and charm of its early pine natural woodwork. From the very moment one steps inside the simple doorway, to glimpse the winding stair turn disappearing round the bend back of the original wide brown boards that shelter it—till one leaves it again with a last backward look, this hallway entrance—which is here reduced to its ultimate minima of attributes—remains nevertheless wholly gratifying merely from its inherent structural integrity, straightforwardness, and obvious fitness and fineness of proportion throughout.

The adjoining living room-kitchen is equally satisfying—and even more appropriate and perfect in its fitments and equipment; rugs, furniture, ironwork,

cupboard—taken down from upstairs in this same house. The old sinkroom, has been changed into a more modernly useful breakfast room, with the gleam of pewter furbishing up its old wall dresser; and beside it the tiny yet satisfyingly proportioned and detailed small bedroom, off the main living room, from beside the fire.

And then upstairs, the more dignified and almost pretentious comfort of a guest bedroom, with its own paneled end, vying in beauty and completeness with its lower floor counterpart—and with a cornice mold even to better it, belike! And it is here, where the interior aspect of the simple dormer is so consistently simple and satisfying, that it is born in upon the beholder that it can hardly have been so well carried out if it had not been original to the house—as they so seldom are.

How sad it is that so few have come down to our time unaltered and unchanged. Their very simplicity and apparent humbleness has made them peculiarly the victims of circumstance, and the unintelligent owner. They have so often fallen into most unfeeling hands. No record of their existence and history has usually been kept. Only occasionally have we exact knowledge of their early owners, or their dates of origin.

Stairway
OLD TARR HOMESTEAD, ROCKPORT,
CAPE ANN, MASSACHUSETTS

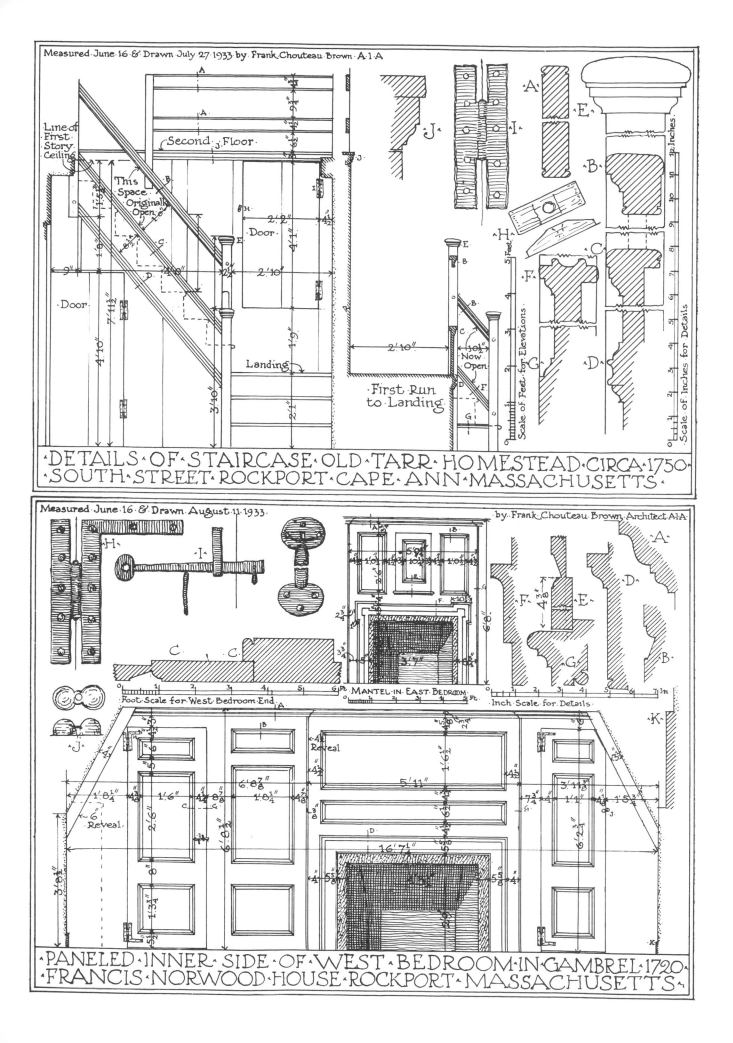

Line of First Story Ceiling

Second Floor

This Space Originally Open

Door

Door

Landing

First Run to Landing

Now Open

Scale of Feet for Elevations

Scale of Inches for Details

·DETAILS·OF·STAIRCASE·OLD·TARR·HOMESTEAD·CIRCA·1750·
·SOUTH·STREET·ROCKPORT·CAPE·ANN·MASSACHUSETTS·

Mantel in East Bedroom

Foot Scale for West Bedroom End

Inch Scale for Details

Reveal

Reveal

·PANELED·INNER·SIDE·OF·WEST·BEDROOM·IN·GAMBREL·1720·
·FRANCIS·NORWOOD·HOUSE·ROCKPORT·MASSACHUSETTS·

Paneled Inner Side of West Bedroom

FRANCIS ("RED CAP") NORWOOD HOUSE—1700-1720—OVERLOOKING HARBOR, ROCKPORT, MASSACHUSETTS

Paneled End of Living Room

FRANCIS ("RED CAP") NORWOOD HOUSE—1700-1720—ROCKPORT, CAPE ANN, MASSACHUSETTS

Living Room Mantel Breast

South Room Mantel Breast

OLD POOLE COTTAGE—1750-1760—ROCKPORT, CAPE ANN, MASSACHUSETTS

Living Room

OLD TARR HOMESTEAD, 6 SOUTH STREET, ROCKPORT, CAPE ANN, MASSACHUSETTS

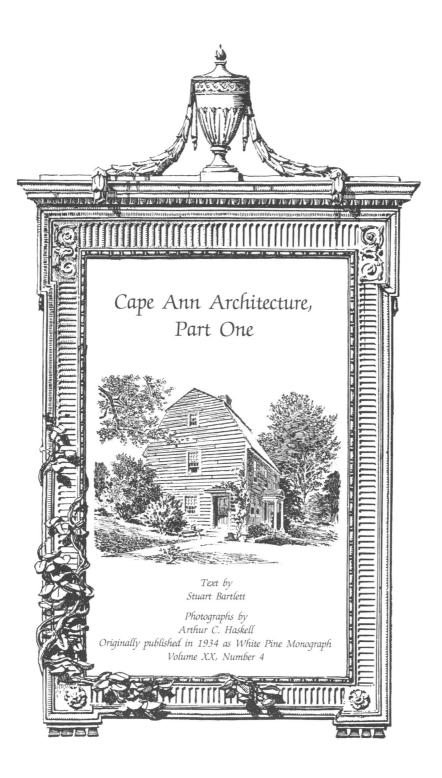

Cape Ann Architecture,
Part One

Text by
Stuart Bartlett

Photographs by
Arthur C. Haskell
Originally published in 1934 as White Pine Monograph
Volume XX, Number 4

GEORGE GOTT HOUSE—1805—9 GOTT STREET, ROCKPORT, MASSACHUSETTS

THE LATER DWELLING ARCHITECTURE OF CAPE ANN, PART ONE

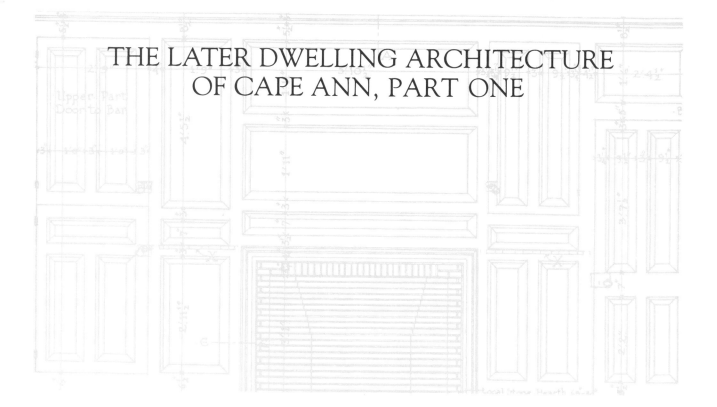

SOME of the simplest yet more dignified examples of these later dwellings are to be found on that portion of the Cape now known as Rockport, which name was given it in 1840, when it was finally set off as a separate town from the then flourishing granite quarries at Pigeon Cove. Previous to that time the district had been known as Sandy Bay, or was merely called the Cape and had been part of Gloucester town since its earliest settlement.

It lies on the eastern part of the Cape, covering an area of about six and one-quarter miles, and is divided into three sections. The North Village, also known as Pigeon Cove, contains the principal quarries; and its old buildings will be described in the final chapter of this volume. In summer it includes the largest part of the transient population of the region. At the other extremity, towards Straitsmouth and Lands End, is the section known as the South End. This, too, has been largely covered in Volume III, Chapter 10.

There remains only the "Center" where, among the many jetties and wharves, covered with fishermen's shacks and artists' studios; the winding streets leading up the rocky slopes to the higher inland country of the Cape, with their old and new houses and cottages, are to be found those few dignified and simple "later houses" remaining on this part of Cape Ann. As a rule these houses were the product of the early

fishing industry (at one time two-thirds of the fishing vessels of Cape Ann belonged in Rockport) but one of the most conspicuous of the town's late houses is the mansion built in 1809 by the Reverend David Jewett, the second minister of what is now the First Parish Church. It is a simple yet distinguished four-chimney square type of dwelling.

Probably next in importance among the houses in that locality is the Caleb Norwood, Jr., House (one of at least six Norwood Houses in Rockport), standing at the beginning of the slope, at 37 Cove Hill. It belongs to the three-story type of house that was produced in a number of the more prosperous Massachusetts coast communities, few of which are older than the last quarter of the eighteenth century.

Nearly opposite, upon a modest street running away from the Harbor, are the two "twin" Gott houses. They are nearly alike in exterior arrangement and exhibit only minor variations of detail, as will appear from a comparison of the two doorways, although the plans and interior details vary. As a matter of fact, Number 5, the second one to be built, now appears to be the older, possibly largely from the fact that it still possesses the inside sliding shutters usually found in much older dwellings.

A little further up the hill leading toward the South End (and so impatient to arrive there that it changes its name no less than four times within a short half-mile of length!) is another remaining Gott Mansion, built in 1770 by one John Gott. This, too, is one of the six or seven three-story dwellings in Rockport, although the upper story was actually added at a later time. The house is of unusual plan, with several staircases and two fireplaces.

Another of the so-called Norwood Houses is the Ebenezer Pool House, fronting upon the famous Dock Square, almost at the beginning of Bear Skin Neck (now usually spelled the other way!) where artists, bathers, and models cluster so thickly on hot summer days.

the first permanent settlements appear to have been made—the region of Annisquam and West Gloucester —so are the greater number of examples of the more prosperous later periods to be found still about the irregular borders of the harbor of Gloucester itself. Here, at one time, were all the houses of the wealthy sea captains or owners of the sailing vessels that then were tied up between voyages at piers located at the water end of the gardens, down which their owners looked from their front doorways on the land side above. At that time the present Main Street of Gloucester did not exist. At a much later date it was cut ruthlessly through the old gardens and front

REV. DAVID JEWETT HOUSE—1806–1809—MAIN STREET, ROCKPORT, MASSACHUSETTS

It is upon this same square that the old Tavern, with its basement taproom and second-story ballroom (added in 1838), still stands; although now, alas, the ballroom has been divided into many rooms, and the old archway through which the coaches drove into the inner courtyard has been filled in with a modern shop. It has still more recently become the headquarters of the artists of the vicinity; and who better than they can appreciate the advantages of restoring the former picturesqueness and appeal of this one-time center of community life on this portion of Cape Ann!

Just as the earliest examples of dwellings within the Cape area are still to be found on that portion where

yards of the big houses perched upon the higher ground above. For a time they were still entered through the old front doorways facing toward the harbor; with a shortened yard, and new fences with gateways and paths leading up from the new street below. Upon the other side of this street lay the warehouses and piers; and gradually business began to encroach upon the land side of the street, with stores built upon the lower ends of the gardens; until today the newer Main Street is banked almost solidly along both sides with stores and business blocks, leaving a few of the old houses to be approached through store passageways or small entrance alleys; or forcing

CALEB NORWOOD, JR., HOUSE — 1775–1780 — ROCKPORT, MASSACHUSETTS

those located still higher upon the bank to turn about for entrance access to the next higher street paralleling the harbor, through a new or old doorway upon the former rear, or side, of the old dwelling.

The Sargent-Murray-Gilman-Hough House is an example of this progress, except that it has here gone even a step farther; and, of still *more* recent years, the families preserving the house have been able to purchase again the land fronting upon Main Street, and have torn down the new stores and built a new fence, so that it is once again possible to view the front of the house upon its Harbor side. For many years

bined leaders, the house has been reclaimed, and with surprisingly little change or necessary repair has been placed in a condition where its innate beauty and charm of detail can be seen and appreciated by visitors.

Of course, it has followed that the years of prosperity of the fishing and other related industries in Gloucester has been the cause of the destruction of most all the old houses that once bordered its inner harbor. One still remains, and is used as an Old Ladies' Home; a few others, further away from the more bustling business section of the Main Street, still exist precariously, but only on sufferance, as tene-

EBENEZER POOL HOUSE — 1798 — DOCK SQUARE, ROCKPORT, MASSACHUSETTS

this noble house stood unregarded in the town. It was a tenement for some time, and only a few knew the beauties of the finish its humble rear exterior concealed. Then it was discovered that John Murray, a minister of the beautiful church built in 1806, and still standing, had once lived in this house. He had married Judith Sargent, daughter of Winthrop Sargent, who was also an ancestor of the late artist, the lamented John Singer Sargent. Aided by those interested in the lives of these two rather strangely com-

ments; often rebuilt, so that many would not even suspect their former magnificence.

Almost beside the Sawyer Free Library stands the old Mackenzie House at 90 Middle Street, built about 1759, with an unusual treatment about the entrance door. As Middle Street continues its course around the harbor toward the main waterfront, it leads by other houses with exterior and interior beauty, as well as architectural details to commend them to the trained and appreciative eye. One of these is the Capt.

Doorway
5 GOTT STREET (GOTT HOUSE)—1806—ROCKPORT, MASSACHUSETTS

Doorway—7 Gott Street
GEORGE GOTT HOUSE—1805—ROCKPORT, MASSACHUSETTS

Doorway
83 MAIN STREET, ROCKPORT, MASSACHUSETTS

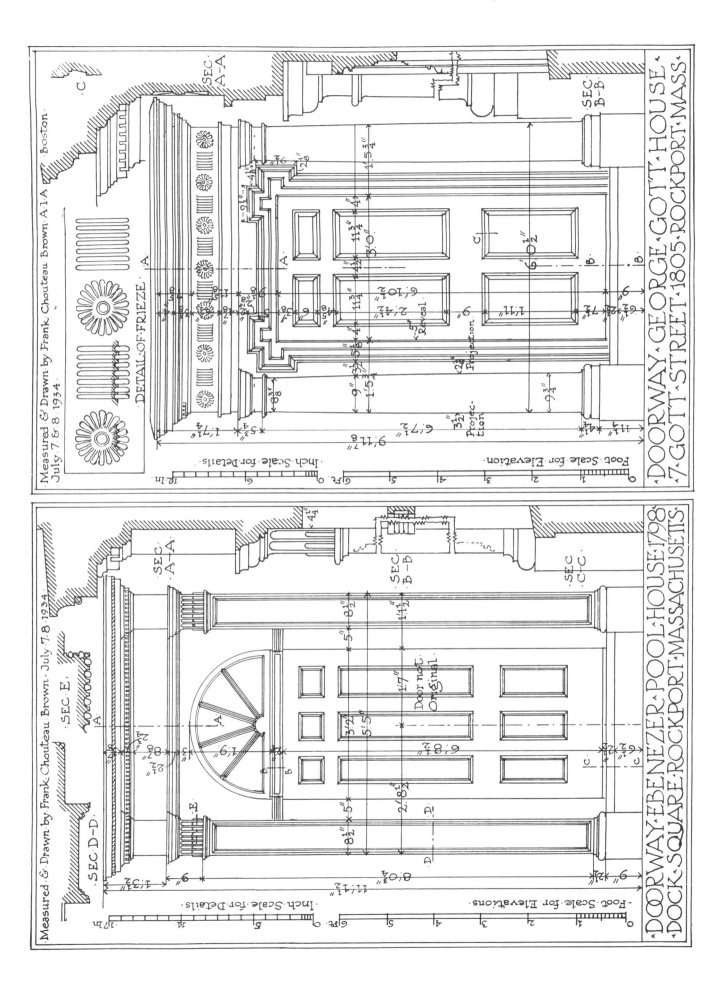

Measured & Drawn by Frank Chouteau Brown · A·I·A · Boston.
July 7 & 8 1934

·DETAIL·OF·FRIEZE·

SEC.
A-A

SEC.
B-B

Inch Scale for Details

Foot Scale for Elevation

·DOORWAY·GEORGE·GOTT·HOUSE·
·7·GOTT·STREET·1805·ROCKPORT·MASS·

Measured & Drawn by Frank Chouteau Brown · July 7. 8. 1934

SEC. E.

SEC.
A-A

SEC.
B-B

SEC.
C-C

SEC. D-D.

Door not original.

Inch Scale for Details

Foot Scale for Elevations

·DOORWAY·EBENEZER·POOL·HOUSE·1798·
·DOCK·SQUARE·ROCKPORT·MASSACHUSETTS·

John Somes House, with its very characteristic door-way design, shown in the photograph on page 194. These entrances were chosen for measuring—in connection with these house designs—because they display some of the most individual and local treatments—that recur again and again, within the region covered by this chapter. This doorway shows the deeply indented and boldly jogged treatment of the architrave surrounding the door. It will be found to appear in many other of the illustrations of this and the succeeding chapter. Also, it illustrates the boldness of reveal and freedom of handling of well known and understood classical models. A close study of these drawings will show how often the use of a hackneyed or conventional detail of the strict order-formula has been adroitly and successfully avoided. In this very entrance the top of the grooves in the triglyph are ended unusually; the door architrave, cornice, and molded edge (A) of the bracket are not the conventional sections. In the Rockport

doorways the details of the pilaster capitals, panels, and molded entablature are at once unusually simple, delicate, and precise—while the jogged and broken outlines around the door frame of the Gott doorway re-echo that local peculiarity, at the same time that the carved ornamental treatment along the frieze is an unusually well worked out variant of an often used and favorite local model.

Thirty years ago both Rockport and Gloucester contained double or triple the number of examples of interesting Colonial dwelling architecture that they contain today. From Gloucester, particularly, have they vanished—though sometimes they may still be suspected of lurking behind modernly reshingled exterior walls, and the outlines of one of the very oldest houses in the district may still be tantalizingly traced under the exterior camouflage of a plastered and half-timbered face-wall treatment that may be found at the now well-named corner of "Pest House Lane"!

GOTT HOUSE—1770—2 PLEASANT STREET, ROCKPORT, MASSACHUSETTS

HOUSE AT 15 HIGH STREET—1800–1820—ROCKPORT, MASSACHUSETTS

SARGENT-MURRAY-GILMAN-HOUGH HOUSE — 1768 — GLOUCESTER, MASSACHUSETTS

MACKENZIE HOUSE — 1760-1790 — MIDDLE STREET, GLOUCESTER, MASSACHUSETTS

Doorway
MACKENZIE HOUSE — 1760 — GLOUCESTER, MASSACHUSETTS

BABSON HOUSE — 1740 — GLOUCESTER, MASSACHUSETTS

OLD COLLINS HOUSE — 1740 — 254 MAIN STREET, GLOUCESTER, MASSACHUSETTS

Doorway — 20 *and* 22 *Middle Street*
CAPT. JOHN SOMES HOUSE — 1800 — GLOUCESTER, MASSACHUSETTS

Doorway
301 and 303 WASHINGTON STREET — 1780 — GLOUCESTER

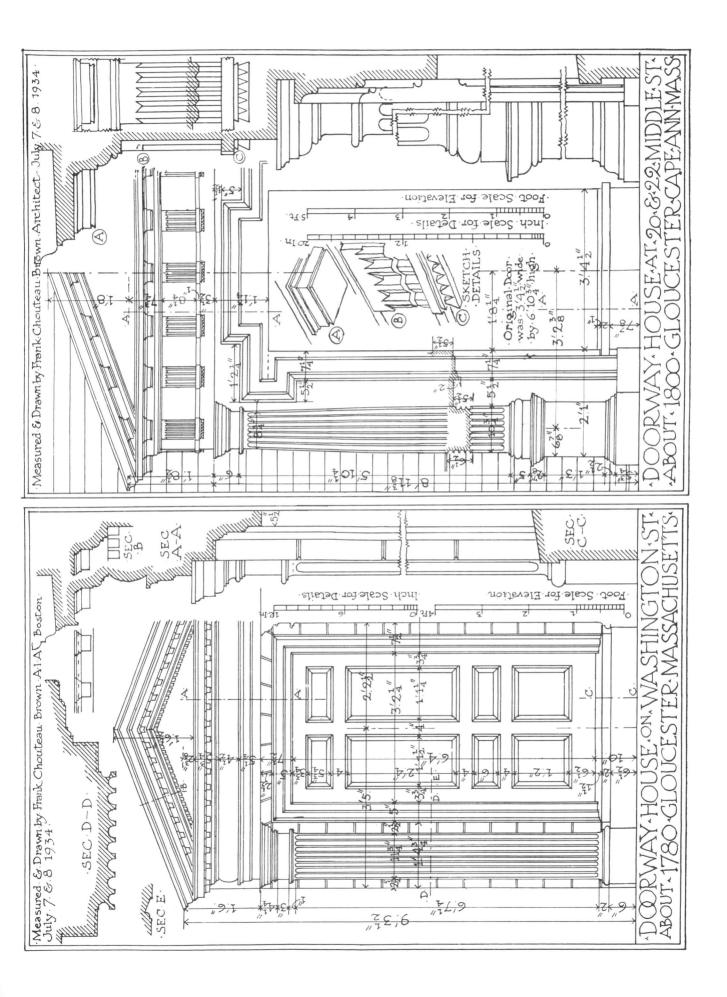

·DOORWAY·HOUSE·AT·20·&·22·MIDDLE·ST·
·ABOUT·1800·GLOUCESTER·CAPE·ANN·MASS·

·DOORWAY·HOUSE·ON·WASHINGTON·ST·
·ABOUT·1780·GLOUCESTER·MASSACHUSETTS·

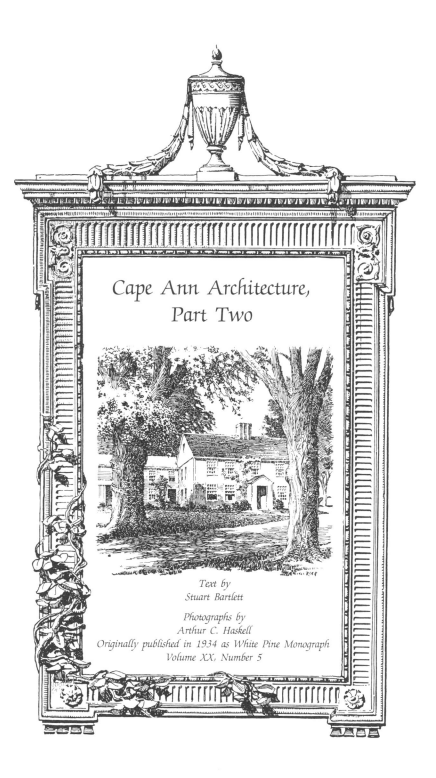

Cape Ann Architecture,
Part Two

Text by
Stuart Bartlett

Photographs by
Arthur C. Haskell
Originally published in 1934 as White Pine Monograph
Volume XX, Number 5

Mantel Detail
MACKENZIE HOUSE — 1760 — GLOUCESTER, MASSACHUSETTS

THE LATER DWELLING ARCHITECTURE OF CAPE ANN, PART TWO

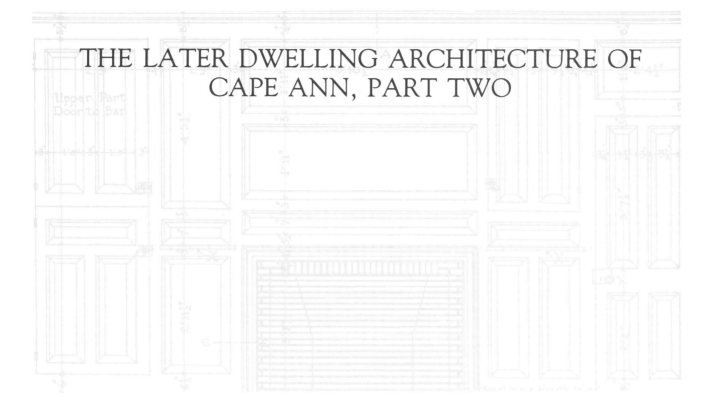

THE better houses still to be found upon the tip of the Cape—or in the region about Rockport Harbor—fall into two general divisions. There is one group about which the legend of "Pirate Gold" persists as the explanation of the source from which the wealth to build them derived—but, alluring as these syllables always are in their appeal, there seems little reason for believing such easily acquired wealth to have been used in their construction—or, if such was actually the case, the dwellings themselves remain as evidence that the source to which their being is still ascribed was hardly as prolific and profitable a one as is usually believed; for they remain as examples of a very simple, direct type of architectural design; quite such as might have been made from the slower and more hardily earned wealth secured from the early fishing fleet that formerly sailed from Rockport and Pigeon Cove; which the buildings themselves would seem to prove to be products of the busy and skillful handiwork of the boatbuilders of that section, as well.

As a matter of actual fact, the better houses of the later period—from about 1760 to 1825—today to be seen in Rockport; are far more expressive of the simplicity and reserve of the New Englanders that created and paid for them, than of any exuberant and flamboyant Pirate spirits! Their interior finish is also of the simplest. Mantels with delicately moulded and sometimes chisel-cut ornament upon a few surfaces. Staircases with simple square posts of small size, the

balusters usually only of the plain seven-eighths or inch-and-an-eighth square type, with a simple but delicate end bracket, are rather the rule. Thin six panel doors, with small moulded panel edges, and a simple mitred architrave. Occasionally a reeded dado-cap above a single wide pine board appears briefly—but the full paneled ends, with sturdy moulded-edge panels, have gone with the earlier period work; and have not persisted into the later period upon this side of the Cape.

Then there are a few unusual examples of a still later style; expressive of the wealth that was briefly derived from the granite quarries that were for some years worked extensively along this coast. This period has expressed itself best perhaps in the several dwellings built of split granite—usually laid up in courses. There remain some barns and outbuildings, a few houses, and one "double cottage"; all built in granite, between about 1825 to 1850. And the interior finish of these houses also continues in carrying on the later simple traditions, established in the immediately preceding period. And within this same time-period lie the few Neo-Grec houses scattered about the region; of which four almost exactly alike in design still remain—two in the Rockport-Pigeon Cove region and two in Gloucester.

Turn to the later settlements, built along the Gloucester harborside, and a quite different story is to be found. Here the lumber industry that had first brought wealth to the settlers upon the rough shores of the Cape, had been supplanted by the fishermen who took up and followed that industry when the earlier fleets of smaller vessels that had previously sailed from Annisquam and Rockport harbors were supplanted by these larger vessels with their homeport in the well protected and deeper waters of the Gloucester Bay.

The old buildings of Gloucester have suffered, particularly, by its prosperity and continued business importance. It remains the "shire" town of the region; and so it has been inevitable that as its business has continued to prosper, its older houses have been more and more altered, or adapted to other uses. Many have been turned into stores; others in not quite so busy a neighborhood have merely fallen into disuse or been made into tenements; while still others, in what have remained better neighborhoods, are now owned by wealthy families—or summer people, and as such, have often been "improved" or "modernized" beyond repair or even sometimes recognition!

Of all these dwellings, the house that was for years the most pretentious and beautiful, was probably that now used as the Sawyer Free Library. Unfortunately, even before it came into the possession of the Library, it had already been much changed and "modernized." The old fence of high wooden pickets that at one time surrounded it, has been taken down and replaced with a costly (and most inartistic) arrangement of cut granite blocks in large sizes; the old paneled and recessed windows have had their sizes enlarged, the sills cut down, and some of the finish changed or removed. The two rooms at the left of the entrance have been entirely torn out, with the old chimney between them, and the finish lost. But of the other front room enough remains to make it an imposing and interesting interior still; though the mantel has been changed. The old staircase is also in place, with the former elaborate landing window, although new rooms have been built behind it.

Across the side street the Mackenzie House still possesses two beautiful paneled ends, on the two right-hand rooms, one above the other; both very similar in design. The second floor room is the one shown on page 198. Again an unusual staircase, and other nice mantels and paneling, remain. Another house across the street (this time across Middle Street) from the Library, is the Murray-Sargent-Gilman-Hough dwelling. It has been preserved as the home of the founder of Universalism— the first church used by John Murray's congregation having been a small building upon another part of this lot, later replaced by the beautiful church built in 1806 that is still standing nearby. This house also has—in two second floor rooms—paneling nearly alike in design along the fireplace sides of the rooms; which are against the outer walls; the end windows occurring only in what are closets,

back of the doors shown in the panelwork! The parlor mantel is quite different from anything else upon the Cape; while the staircase, although painted, is one of the best examples of the elaborate twisted type in New England; although not done in mahogany—as in the Lee Mansion at Marblehead. The hallway and front rooms of this house were built, along with the kitchen ell and the odd corner fireplace upon the second floor over it, in 1768.

Both these houses are of rather an early date; as is even more true of the well known Babson House, which contains one of the most beautiful all-paneled rooms in the state (and one of the two still remaining upon Cape Ann!) with a most interesting staircase. This house also exhibits three old vestibule entrances, and a modern porch upon the garden front.

The Old Collins House—now descended to use as a tenement and a storehouse of odds and ends of fishing tackle—had once seen better days as the home of a ship owner facing down upon the heel of the harbor. It still stands in its old location, now closely hemmed in with stores upon right and left, huddled up against the rocky hillside, as always. A sturdy old staircase and the dominating vigor and boldness of its best rooms are worthy of better things.

Just as Rockport boasts of its "twin" Gott houses; so has Gloucester also a pair of "twins"; and also built—according to the legend—by two brothers. These two buildings on Pleasant St. were, however, being carried along at the same time—and a certain amount of rivalry was in evidence between both the workmen and the owners; each striving to in some way better the design or workmanship over its competitor (a somewhat different spirit than nowadays dominates the thoughts and ideals of the members of our building "Unions"!) and the story goes that, one morning, the owner of one house, having already nailed up his cornerboards, and rushed the wall clapboarding along ahead of his competitor, arrived upon the scene to find that Col. Jacob Smith "housewright" —his apparently slower neighbor—had been spending the time more elaborately grooving his corner boards into a sort of elaborate quoining—rather unusually small in scale—and was even then setting them up into place! "And," as the story goes, dramatically, "he gave one look at them and turned away and never spoke another word to him, from that day to this!" And it is this—the more elaborate of the two houses —that is now the home of the Cape Ann Scientific, Literary and Historical Association (all of which is merely long for Historical Society). This house dates from 1808; and is an excellent and representative example of that period, as it took shape in the neighborhood and within the area of that rugged and picturesque island that is known as Cape Ann!

Hall and Stairway
SARGENT-MURRAY-GILMAN-HOUGH HOUSE—1768—GLOUCESTER, MASSACHUSETTS

First Floor Parlor

SARGENT-MURRAY-GILMAN-HOUGH HOUSE — 1768 — GLOUCESTER, MASSACHUSETTS

Paneled End in Dining Room Chamber, Second Floor
SARGENT-MURRAY-GILMAN-HOUGH HOUSE—1768—GLOUCESTER, MASSACHUSETTS

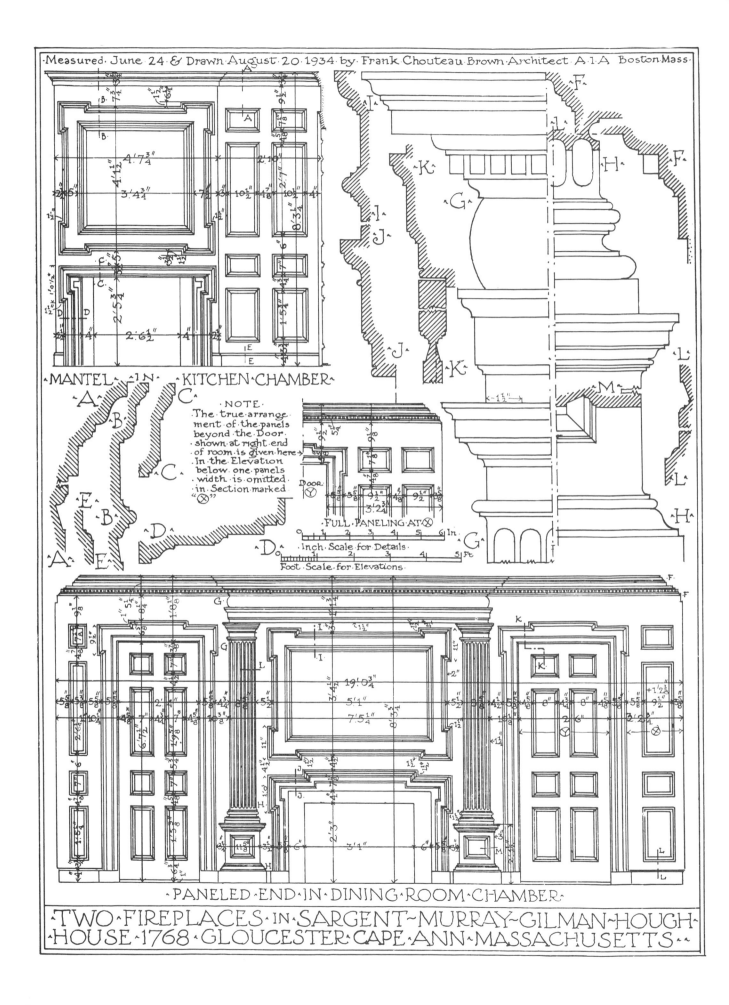

Measured June 24 & Drawn August 20 1934 by Frank Chouteau Brown Architect A.I.A. Boston Mass.

MANTEL · IN · KITCHEN · CHAMBER

· NOTE ·
The true arrangement of the panels beyond the Door shown at right end of room is given here. In the Elevation below one panels width is omitted in Section marked "⊗"

FULL PANELING AT ⊗

Inch Scale for Details
Foot Scale for Elevations

· PANELED · END · IN · DINING · ROOM · CHAMBER ·

· TWO · FIREPLACES · IN · SARGENT ~ MURRAY ~ GILMAN ~ HOUGH ·
· HOUSE · 1768 · GLOUCESTER · CAPE · ANN · MASSACHUSETTS · ~ ·

Mantel in Kitchen Chamber
SARGENT-MURRAY-GILMAN-HOUGH HOUSE — 1768 — GLOUCESTER, MASSACHUSETTS

MACKENZIE HOUSE—1760—90 MIDDLE STREET, GLOUCESTER, MASSACHUSETTS

OLD COLLINS HOUSE—1760–1770—254 MAIN STREET, GLOUCESTER, MASSACHUSETTS

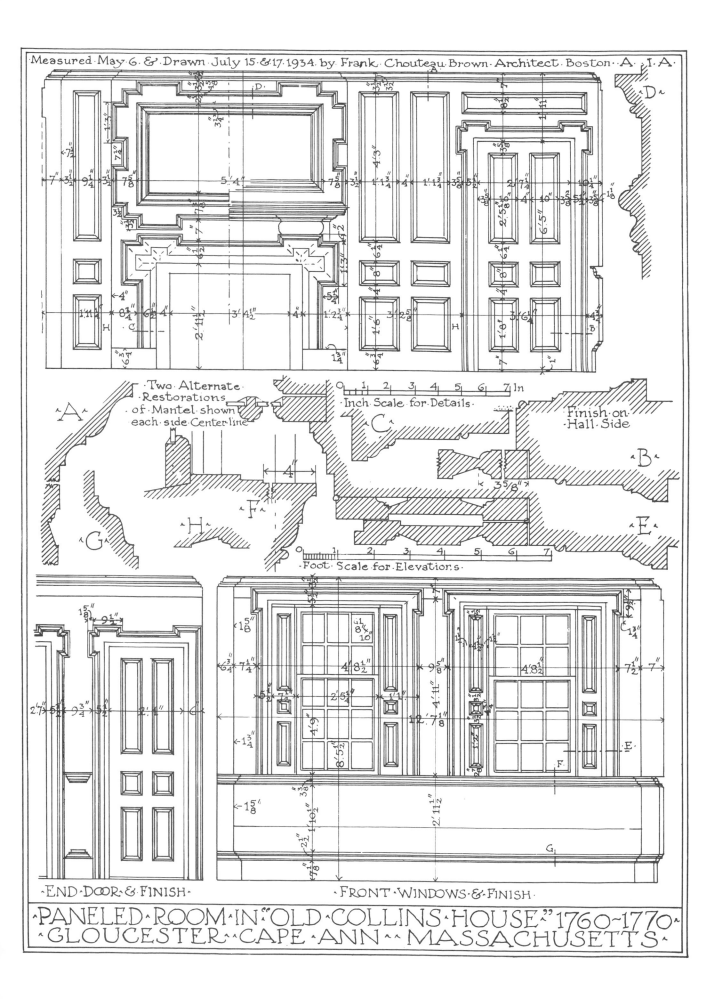

Measured May 6 & Drawn July 15 & 17 1934 by Frank Chouteau Brown Architect Boston A.I.A.

Two Alternate Restorations of Mantel shown each side Center line

Inch Scale for Details

Finish on Hall Side

Foot Scale for Elevations

END DOOR & FINISH

FRONT WINDOWS & FINISH

PANELED ROOM IN "OLD COLLINS HOUSE" 1760-1770
GLOUCESTER CAPE ANN MASSACHUSETTS

Side Window and Finish

Mantel, Panel and Door

PANELED ROOM IN OLD COLLINS HOUSE—1760-1770—GLOUCESTER, CAPE ANN, MASSACHUSETTS

Dining Room

BABSON HOUSE—1740—GLOUCESTER, CAPE ANN, MASSACHUSETTS

Window and Panel Details
BABSON HOUSE—1740—GLOUCESTER, CAPE ANN, MASSACHUSETTS

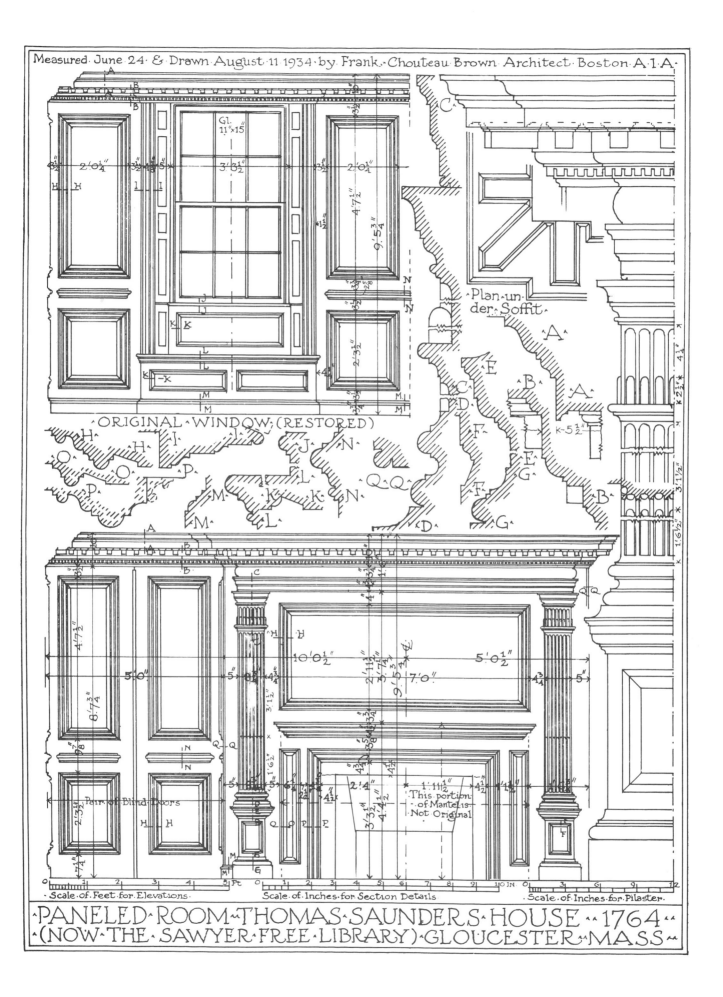

Measured June 24 & Drawn August 11 1934 by Frank Chouteau Brown Architect Boston A.I.A.

Gl. 11"x15"

Plan under Soffit

ORIGINAL WINDOW (RESTORED)

Pair of Blind Doors

This portion of Mantel is Not Original

Scale of Feet for Elevations.   Scale of Inches for Section Details   Scale of Inches for Pilaster.

PANELED·ROOM~THOMAS·SAUNDERS·HOUSE~·1764~·
·(NOW·THE·SAWYER·FREE·LIBRARY)·GLOUCESTER·MASS~

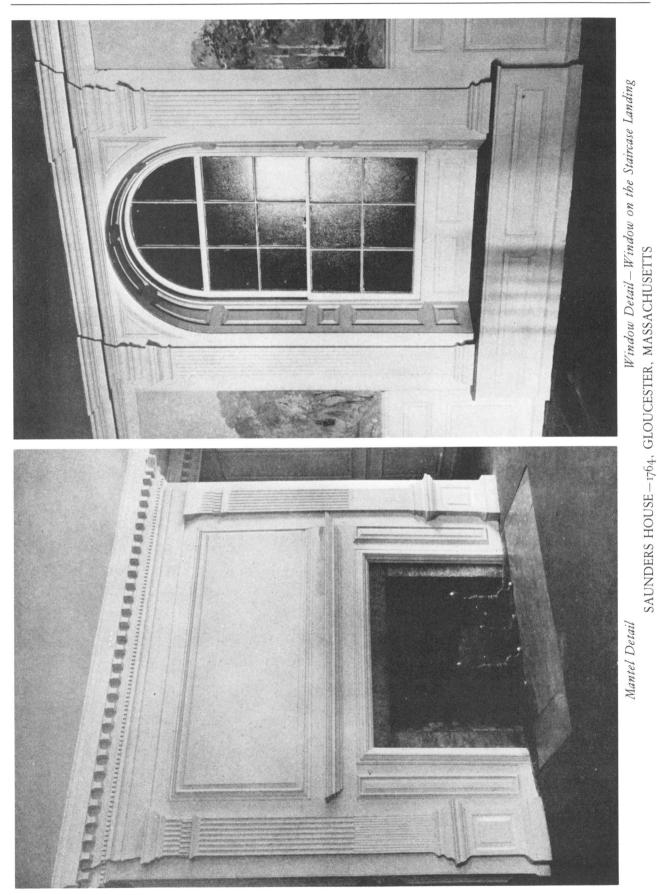

Window Detail—Window on the Staircase Landing

SAUNDERS HOUSE—1764, GLOUCESTER, MASSACHUSETTS
Now the Sawyer Free Library

Mantel Detail

Mantel and Closet Detail
GEORGE GOTT HOUSE—1805—7 GOTT STREET, ROCKPORT,
CAPE ANN, MASSACHUSETTS

Mantel Detail
CAPE ANN SCIENTIFIC, LITERARY, AND HISTORICAL
ASSOCIATION BUILDING—1808—GLOUCESTER, MASSACHUSETTS

Annisquam, Massachusetts

Text by
Frank Chouteau Brown

Photographs by
Arthur C. Haskell
Originally published in 1932 as White Pine Monograph
Volume XIX, Number 1

CAPE ANN: SOME EARLIER COLONIAL DWELLINGS IN AND ABOUT ANNISQUAM, MASSACHUSETTS

AMONG the visual difficulties confronting any-one trying to reconstruct in his imagination a picture of the conditions under which the first settlers in the colonies were compelled to live—conditions that were instrumental in shaping the character and form of the early dwellings first built along its shores—are the false ideas obtained, all too unconsciously, from viewing houses given early dates that are still to be seen in certain localities, particularly in New England.

Therefore the "Pioneer Village," reconstructed upon the margin of Salem Harbor two years ago for the celebration of the Massachusetts Bay Tercentenary, which not only showed several full size examples of the various types of dwellings built during the first few years; but also illustrated the means employed in fashioning lumber, making bricks, obtaining salt, and otherwise securing a precarious livelihood under the most primitive conditions, supplied for the first time a clear and definitely visualized background, against which it was possible for almost anyone to project a self-convincing picture of the lives and customs of the early settlers.

There one can see not only the crude makeshifts of the first winter shelters, but also the first fully constructed or fashioned buildings; as well as the more completely framed and carpentered houses of one and even two stories, which it is quite impossible to find in their original unadorned simplicity in any of the very earliest structures remaining today. Always they carry the date, based upon that portion earliest built,

and now incorporated indistinguishably into a form much enlarged and developed from the aspect that the earliest portion alone had first assumed. And this holds true, even in those rare instances when the existing structure has been properly and authoritatively reft of its increment of generations of minor changes, and restrainedly "restored"!

Considering three hundred years of wear and tear, accompanied by the early and continued dangers of fire, the many Indian wars, the perishable and often hastily and inexpertly prepared materials of which the houses were compounded; and the primitive and sometimes unskilled manner in which materials were early employed, it is certainly not surprising that so few very early buildings exist to show the true type of primitive Colonial dwelling, but rather the surprising part is that we can still point to any examples at all!

Perhaps the Peak House in Medfield still provides us with one of the best pictures of the early dwelling, with the Blake House in Dorchester (1648) for an illustration of its immediately succeeding type. But certainly in the older portion of the Riggs House, in Riverdale, on Cape Ann, we can today secure the best idea that is possible of one of these earliest type houses. The Alexander Standish House (Duxbury, 1666) and the William Harlow House (Plymouth, 1677) are both gambrel roofed; and, as such, are undoubtedly in the second manner—quite similar to the "newer part" of the Riggs House, as it appears herewith. The first built Riggs dwelling was a two-room house of roughly squared logs, laid horizontally one on top of the other, making a wall about 15 inches thick. A roof of rather steep pitch was added, unbroken by any windows until about twenty years ago, when a dormer was cut into the roof on the side toward the water. The gambrel portion was added at the west end of the earlier house about forty years later.

As soon as a fully framed structure was attempted it was natural that the New England settlers should turn to the medieval type of timber-framed dwelling, with which they had been familiar at home, as a model for their construction in this new country. Consequently, the heavy sill-and-cornerpost frame, with plate and girt mortised and held with oak pins, came naturally into use. When, as at first, beaten earth was used as the floor, the sill was merely laid upon this base, or a few flat stones were placed at the corners or along the length for better support. The "raised sills" showing above the floor levels in a few houses (no less than four such may still be seen about Cape Ann) are a survival from this very time.

These framed structural outlines were then boarded upon the outside, usually with inch or inch-and-a-quarter thick boards, running perpendicularly from sill to plate or gable rafter ends; and pinned or nailed to the larger horizontal timbers, with small studdings used only to frame around a door or window opening. Sometimes these boards were tongued and grooved and molded at the edges; sometimes they were merely set close together and the spaces between filled with mud or clay, lime mortar or plaster.

The one-story house has often only one or two rooms upon the lower floor with an attic overhead, frequently left undivided. (Indeed, it is usually still found in this latter condition in many cottages along the coast, or inland in the country, built from a hundred to a hundred and fifty years ago!) At first access to this attic was by scuttle and ladder; replaced a little later by a steep stair running sharply up from beside the hall, or in the front entry.

The chimney was the most important part of these early houses. Built of stone or brick, set in mud or lime shell mortar, it was usually located at one end of these simpler types of dwellings, which were then most naturally enlarged by adding another room or two beyond the chimney, thus at once obtaining access to it and doubling the house in length. The next enlargement usually took the form of a long rear lean-to; with possible other later additions develop-

RIGGS HOUSE—1660–1700—RIVERDALE, CAPE ANN, MASSACHUSETTS

RIGGS HOUSE—1660–1700—RIVERDALE, CAPE ANN, MASSACHUSETTS

ing as end "ells" or further lean-tos increasing the length of the structure, sometimes to a very considerable extent.

Possibly the favorite means of enlarging the early houses, however, was by leaving the older portion, nearly undisturbed, to serve as a kitchen ell; and adding a new—and very much larger house—usually at one or the other end. Sometimes this was done, as in the Riggs House here shown, by continuing the new part in length along the same frontage as the old, which almost invariably faced to the south. Sometimes it was added either at an angle, or quite at right angles to the older structure, the new front then often being to the east or west. This later method was perhaps often adopted from the fact that it was by this means possible to face the house anew upon the road; which had probably been built long after the original cottage had been informally placed facing south across some pleasant pasture, or looking out upon some livelier water view.

Thomas Riggs, "scrivener," the second Town Clerk of Gloucester and its first Schoolmaster, settled on Cape Ann at Goose Cove, in 1658, and built the

pitch-roof portion of the present dwelling of squared pine logs 15 inches thick, probably shortly previous to the year 1660. The gambrel part was added by a grandson, George Riggs, about 1700. This dwelling still stands in Vine Street, near the Riverdale Willows, only a short distance beyond Church Green, which is just north and at the back of the well known White-Ellery House, generally dated as 1703 or 1704, but probably built nearer 1710. This was the parsonage of the first minister, Rev. John White, of the Parish Church that stood across the Green. From 1738 onward it was used as a Tavern, or Ordinary, by James Stevens and his successors. One of the first houses in the Massachusetts Bay Colony (though not actually erected on Cape Ann) was the Community House, the materials for which were brought over from England. It stood just across on the mainland, in that part of Gloucester known as Stage Fort Park; and was afterwards removed and re-erected in Naumkeag, now Salem.

Another early house nearby was built for the home of Richard Dike or Dyke. A date as early as 1643 has been claimed for this dwelling; but it was more

Fireplace
RIGGS HOUSE — 1660–1700 — RIVERDALE, MASSACHUSETTS

Staircase — First Floor
DYKE-WHEELER HOUSE — 1668 — GLOUCESTER, MASSACHUSETTS

HARRADEN HOUSE — 1657 — ANNISQUAM, MASSACHUSETTS

Paneled Room End

DYKE-WHEELER HOUSE — c1668 — GLOUCESTER, MASSACHUSETTS

probably built much nearer 1668, at which time this property—with a dwelling upon it—was transferred to John Fitch. It was again sold in 1714 to John Colt; and the pleasantly proportioned paneling of the principal room, and the stairway, are probably both from this or an even later date. Bought by Finson Wheeler in 1834, it has been known by that name ever since; and has now been somewhat modified to serve the purposes of a summer cottage, which it does excellently well.

Most of the historical background of the early years of Cape Ann best relate to the history of its largest city, Gloucester. But those who know it only for that picturesque, overbuilt area surrounding the irregular shores of its busy harbor; or for the summer reaches of its rocky moorlands from Eastern Point through Bass Rocks to Land's End; or even the teeming artist colonies of Rockport and Bearskin Neck, can know little or nothing of old Annisquam, oldest settlement of all the Cape. And indeed, few do know much about this sleepy little settlement, stretched out along the landlocked waters of the Cove. The casual sightseer, touring around the Cape, passes it entirely by; as does also the usual summer sojourner, going back and forth between the summer colonies fronting westerly across Ipswich Bay and the stations at Gloucester or Rockport. To feel its old-world charm one must turn aside from the main highway, down a narrow lane coming out upon the "floating bridge" that crosses the mouth of the Cove, or if coming from Bay View, swing sharply right back of the church at its innermost tip, so continuing along the narrow winding Leonard Street, from which circuitous lanes lead backward and forward, bending around rock outcrops, old stone benches and huge butternut trees to connect with backyards of places fronting the waterway, or reach the much-used side doors of houses whose fronts overhang other inner yards, or overlook low-lying roofs to the far wind-blown stretches of Winnegoeschieke—formerly Coffin's—Beach.

Embowered in the long untrimmed verdure of thick hedges, or heavily limbed low-hanging trees, many an old house lies quietly sleping and hidden, a mere gravel-toss from a practicable street; that may nevertheless end unexpectedly—and somewhat suddenly—at the water's edge; or against a heavy sea wall; or merely die out of existence between two or three old fenced yards and as many angularly sloping cottages, helter-skelterly faced to any and all points of the boxable compass.

On this limited, and irregular area, between 1631 and 1633, a few men and families from Plymouth effected the first permanent settlement on Cape Ann. Meanwhile the fishing at Gloucester was being estab-

lished and that town was finally incorporated in 1642. The same year, according to early records, a building boom was the cause of setting up a sawmill at Riverdale, which was about midway between Annisquam and Gloucester. Aided by the output of this mill, the second generation of settlers covered their early squared log houses with clapboards, laid sawed board floors, and applied split shingles over end wall boarding and on roof scantlings.

The first permanent settlers at Annisquam were made into the Third Parish in 1728, while the third meeting house of the First Parish had been raised on Meeting House Green in May of 1700, being described as "a building 40 by 40, with 16-foot posts, plastered with lime and hair," and costing £253.

Meanwhile the early simpler square little houses, scattered about Riverdale and Annisquam, were being lengthened and enlarged, "raised" to an added story height; and soon—near the end of the seventeenth century—a few four-room, full two-story houses were being built. Along the shores of the Cove old single houses with huge chimney at one end were also being lengthened by building another dwelling upon the outer side of the chimney, originally perhaps to house a younger generation of the same family; later to pass by marriage into quite alien hands. A number of old examples of this stand about the Cape, one being what is now known as The Castle, built shortly after 1700 upon the bank of the Cove, with a huge chimney top only to mark its age from the passing roadway, though from the water it may be seen to better advantage.

Nearby is the house built almost as early, the home of Madame Goss, used as officers' quarters in the War of 1812, but now hopelessly changed upon the outside; as is also the case with the Old Tavern, built just before 1700, and used as a soldiers' barracks in 1812. This still stands across the street from the Harraden House. The latter, with its earliest portion built about 1657 for Edward Harraden, one of the first settlers, has since been much changed about, added to, and built over, having now two lean-tos, of different levels, a one- and a two-story section, at the rear.

Continuing along the main street, passing the village center store and post office, and many cottages of age and charm, the little house on the corner of Arlington Street that is reproduced may be seen—and, almost at the Cove's end, the little gambrel house, built probably soon after 1700, that is perhaps the most perfect of all the remaining cottages of modest appeal and venerable age now to be found upon the Cape.

At the Head of the Cove stands the old Church. Although the present building dates only from 1831,

DENNISON HOUSE—1727—SANDY BAY ROAD, ANNISQUAM, MASSACHUSETTS

Paneled Room End—Second Floor
DENNISON HOUSE—1727—ANNISQUAM, MASSACHUSETTS

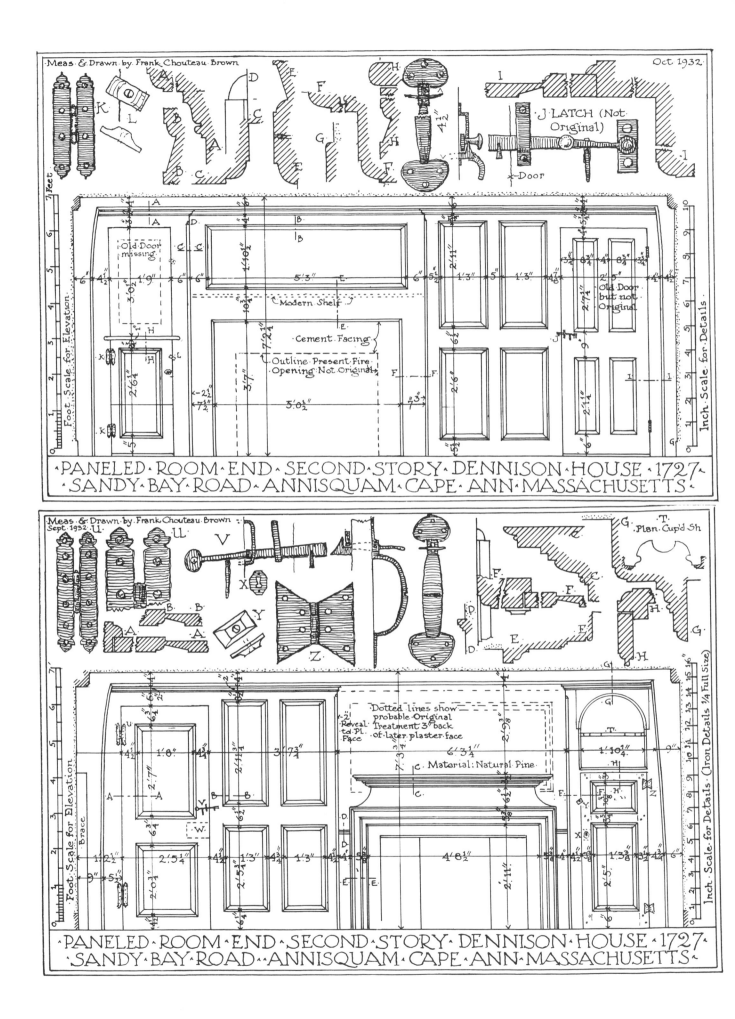

Meas. & Drawn by Frank Chouteau Brown   Oct. 1932

·PANELED·ROOM·END·SECOND·STORY·DENNISON·HOUSE·1727·
·SANDY·BAY·ROAD·ANNISQUAM·CAPE·ANN·MASSACHUSETTS·

Meas. & Drawn by Frank Chouteau Brown
Sept. 1932

·PANELED·ROOM·END·SECOND·STORY·DENNISON·HOUSE·1727·
·SANDY·BAY·ROAD·ANNISQUAM·CAPE·ANN·MASSACHUSETTS·

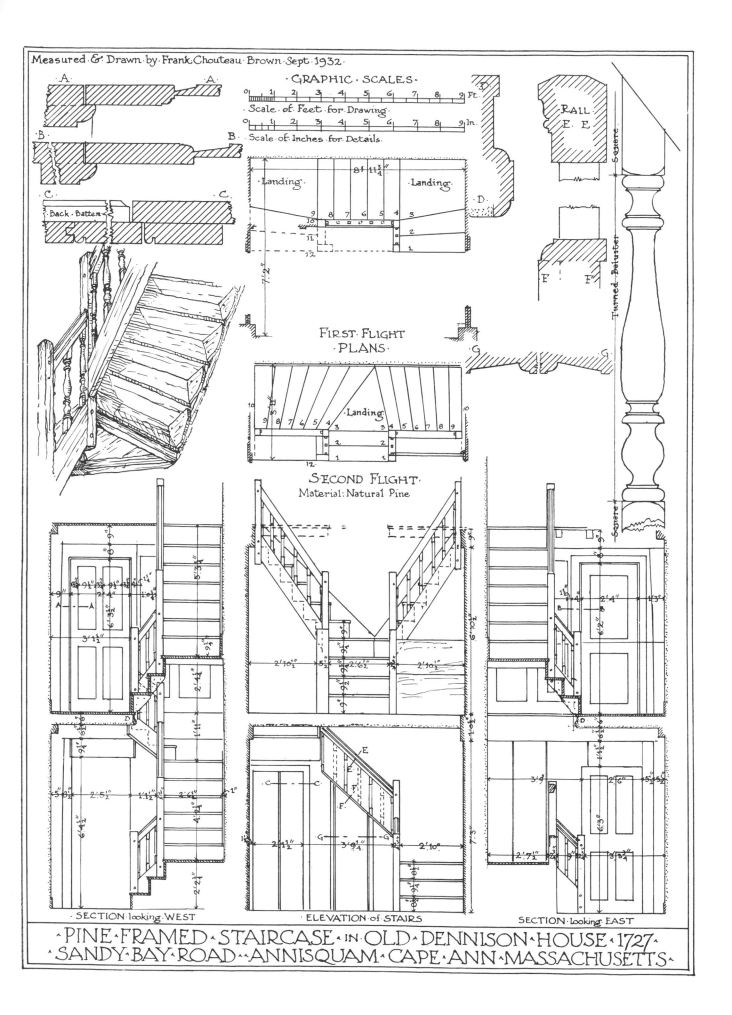

Measured & Drawn by Frank Chouteau Brown Sept. 1932.

A A

·GRAPHIC·SCALES·

RAIL
E E

Scale of Feet for Drawing

B B
· Scale of Inches for Details.

C · Back · Batten · C

Landing · 8½ · 11¾" · Landing · D

·FIRST·FLIGHT·
·PLANS·

7'·2"

·SECOND·FLIGHT·
Material: Natural Pine

Turned Baluster

E E

Square

·SECTION· looking WEST   ·ELEVATION· of STAIRS   ·SECTION· looking EAST

·PINE·FRAMED·STAIRCASE· IN·OLD·DENNISON·HOUSE·1727·
·SANDY·BAY·ROAD·ANNISQUAM·CAPE·ANN·MASSACHUSETTS·

Second Flight

First Flight

Framed Staircase — DENNISON HOUSE — 1727 — ANNISQUAM, MASSACHUSETTS

COTTAGE AT HEAD OF COVE – ABOUT 1700 – ANNISQUAM, MASSACHUSETTS

HOUSE AT CORNER OF ARLINGTON STREET, ANNISQUAM, MASSACHUSETTS

ROBINSON HOMESTEAD — 1710-1715 — LANESVILLE, MASSACHUSETTS

its predecessor was planted there in 1728! — surrounded with a pleasant group of little cottages and one more pretentious house of about 1800 (of all of which more will be heard anon), while nearly across the main roadway, leading up into the interior of the Cape, is the old Sandy Bay Road, now Revere St., leading up to the old quarries and one end of Dog Town Common (and that, too, is another story!).

In a pleasant valley among the woods, at what appears to be the very end of the road, lies the old Dennison House, dating from 1727, though follow-

individuality of some previous owner or tenant. Nevertheless, the views taken show a more than usually interesting staircase, carrying out in natural pine almost exactly the forms of its oak predecessors of fifty years before; the balusters alone, while still of even the earliest outlines, marking the difference. The details of this stairway, as well as its open support underneath, may be studied also in a measured drawing; another sheet shows some of the panelled ends remaining in the rooms. One of these, showing the natural pine, in a bedroom, has also been photo-

WHITE-ELLERY HOUSE — 1703–1710 — GLOUCESTER, MASSACHUSETTS

ing precisely a much earlier style. Although but little known, the place has very recently come into the possession of Mr. Earl Sanborn, who is transferring his Glass Studio to a new structure built in back of the old dwelling, where windows for the new Washington Cathedral are now taking shape.

As yet no attempt has been made to reconstruct or restore the original aspect of the house, or its interiors. Outside, its age is still disguised under a comparatively modern coating of shingles; and every here or there in the interior still appear evidences of the

graphed; with a later, but still finely appealing mantel; and a charming original cupboard. Other panelling has been painted over, and some of the fireplaces filled up, or reduced in size; while the old Hall contains an example of a mantelshelf that, if not an original in date, may have been added soon after, from its simple appropriateness and feeling for relation to the room and its panelling.

Despite its later date, this house is among the earliest in appearance of the few full two-story dwellings on the Cape; and has the earliest type of staircase.

Pigeon Cove, Massachusetts

Text by
Thomas Williams

Photographs by
Arthur C. Haskell
Originally published in 1933 as White Pine Monograph
Volume XIX, Number 4

Garrison House Portion
WITCH HOUSE, PIGEON COVE, MASSACHUSETTS

SOME OLD HOUSES OF PIGEON COVE, MASSACHUSETTS

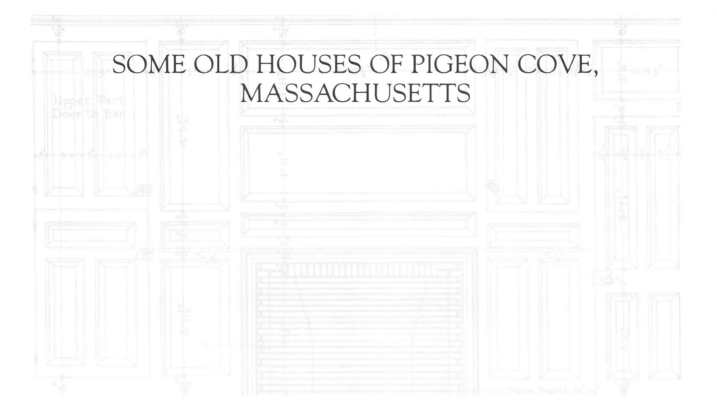

THIRTY miles northeast of Boston, Cape Ann juts out into the ocean, a rocky island of many rocks and ledges. Rather barren inland, with bouldered pastures, swamps, and tangled thickets, its perimeter is settled almost continuously with a series of attractive villages which cluster around the harbors and coves, straggling out along the highway and shore.

Originally the whole cape was in the town of Gloucester, although from early days there were two *nuclei* of settlement. One was built around the harbor, Gloucester, and the "cut" through the marshes which from early days made the cape an island and gave the fishing boats a short and easy passage to Annisquam behind the shelter of the cape. Sandy Bay, on the ocean side of the cape, settled later, became the second and less important center of population, numbering by the time of the Revolution about 400 people.

Sandy Bay organized a separate parish in 1754, and finally in 1840 incorporated as the town of Rockport. Pigeon Cove, whose old houses form the subject of this chapter, is the North Village of Rockport, and includes the ocean shore of the extreme tip of Cape Ann. The cove itself, whose sandy beach was formerly partially sheltered by a dyke of rocks called The Pillions, is now protected by a breakwater which affords complete shelter for many small fishing boats and an occasional coal barge, while the beach has disappeared under the highway and the forge of the Cape Ann Tool Company.

At the opening of the seventeenth century, Sandy Bay and Pigeon Cove presented an appearance far different from that of today. Champlain in 1605 described Rockport and its three islands (later named by Capt. John Smith the Turks' Heads) as heavily wooded. The shore probably closely resembled the wooded portions of the Maine coast today. Many residents remember the last stands of primeval pines in Annisquam, along Goose Cove and around the Old Dennison House (described in Volume III, Chapter 14) which used to bring visitors from miles around until at last they succumbed to the lumberman. Such forests, so convenient to water transportation, from early times attracted the woodcutters, who, toward the end of the seventeenth century, found considerable profit in cutting and selling timber which was transported to Boston, and thence perhaps to England, in sloops loaded at Gap Head and Pigeon Cove.

The town early realized the importance of the timber on the Common land and took steps to conserve it, and at the same time to encourage the development of the infant local shipbuilding and shipping industries. Thus, in 1669, "it was agreed that there should be no cordwood sold out of town under three shillings and sixpence per cord." For several successive years, each family was permitted to cut twenty cords on the town's Common for its own use. In 1698, "Liberty is given to the gentlemen of Boston that is concerned in building a ship heare in the towne of Gloucester to get what timber is needful upon the towne's common land, provided they employ such men of the towne as are capable of working upon the ship." Again, in 1702, certain persons were granted timber from Common land for shipbuilding, but "the said personses is to pay to the towne three shillings pr tunn in case the said S^d Sloop be sold or disposed of out of towne before six years be expired x x." By 1706, in spite of all restrictions, thirty sloops were employed in the timber trade on the inside portion of the Cape alone, a number reduced to eighteen by 1710.

A second important attraction to the early settlers of Cape Ann was the abundance of fish in its surrounding waters. One of the earliest enterprises of the Plymouth Colony was the establishing at Gloucester Harbor in 1624 of a landing stage and the founding of a small settlement to serve as a base for the pursuit of the fishing industry. This effort was doomed to failure, but the settlement of Gloucester remained permanent and was destined to develop the very prosperous fishing industry which is still carried on today.

Of course, trade early became an important occupation in this maritime settlement, whose remoteness also, perhaps, encouraged smuggling. In 1700, the Earl of Bellamont wrote to the Lords of Trade of the unlawful trade of the Colony, "if the merchants of Boston be minded to run their goods there is nothing to hinder them," and "'tis a common thing, as I have heard, to unload their ships at Cape Ann, and bring their goods to Boston in wood-boats."

Records are entirely lacking as to the details of the early settlement of Sandy Bay; although we know that Richard Tarr, who during the last quarter of the seventeenth century built his cabin near what is now Rockport Harbor, was the first permanent settler. It is certain, however, that prior to that time fishermen from Chebacco (now Essex) and Ipswich, towns on the mainland to the northwest, had established posts at Gap Head and Pigeon Cove, built huts, and made these points their temporary abode.

Champlain had found the Indians at "Cap des Isles," as he called Cape Ann, very amiable, although he was much on his guard against them; and later visitors and settlers seem to have had no serious trouble with them. The whole district, however, was terrified of the Indians during King Philip's War, and the Indian attacks came alarmingly close to the towns of Chebacco and Ipswich, whose fishermen were using Gap Head and Pigeon Cove as bases. In March of 1676, spurred on by the peril, a committee of the General Court reported that Cape Ann "had made two garrison houses, besides several particular fortifications."

Back from Pigeon Cove, on the top of a low hill, to the north, stands the Old Garrison House, in more recent years known as the Witch House. Although documentary evidence is lacking, it seems a reasonable assumption that this was built for the protection of woodcutters and fishermen, whose temporary huts offered scant security against Indian raids, and that it was one of the two garrison houses referred to by the Committee of the General Court in 1676. This assumption is borne out by the character of the building, whose exterior walls are of square-hewn logs of hard pine or tamarack, 7 inches thick and strongly dovetailed at the corners; with a second story overhang of about a foot which originally existed on all four sides.

The log construction below this overhang shows such careful workmanship on the very hard wood that the cracks between logs are in many places very difficult to find. Above the second floor level, however, the chinks are quite wide in places, suggesting that the builders may have been hurried by approaching winter.

The framing of the first floor ceiling, which cantilevers out to support the overhang, is very unusual with hard pine beams about five inches by seventeen inches moulded at the edges and laid flat, three on each side of the chimney. The spaces between these beams, about thirty inches, are spanned by the single thickness of 1½-inch floor planks without the aid of joists. The oak end girts and chimney girts, about seven inches wide by twelve inches deep, also cantilever through the walls and help support the overhangs.

The cellar and second floor ceilings are constructed in the usual seventeenth century manner, with summer beam supporting floor joists. The roof is of purlin construction, with vertical boarding.

How crude the original house must have been! With no outside sheathing, unplastered, not even chinked, its occupants were at the mercy of every wind. The primitive character of the original finish is indicated by the fact that, with the possible exception of the plank partition which supports the stair, all of the original interior work has disappeared in the course of many alterations, the first of which must have been begun as soon as the building was permanently occupied. The original chimney also succumbed to some eighteenth century alteration, probably because of inferior construction of underburned bricks and clay mortar.

The restored Fire Room is probably a fairly accurate representation of its original appearance. The hard pine sheathing, though not original, is of the period, and the fireplace and hearth have been rebuilt on their old foundation on the model of a nearby original. The walls have been stripped of later plaster to what was undoubtedly their original state. The addition of the furniture, which is American of the general period of the room, completes the picture, giving us a very unusual opportunity to see how these primitive early rooms really did look.

The living room, the fireplace end of which is illustrated, exhibits simple arrangement of a fireplace and pine doors and trim, which were installed in the early portion of the house in the late eighteenth century.

pedimented doorway (saved from the wreckage of an old Essex mansion) to take the place of the original, which had disappeared. In this eighteenth century ell are the dining room, with its unusual gouge-work over the fireplace, and the chamber with the deep chimney breast.

A series of nineteenth century additions, including the Victorian bay windows, make the house a mixture

THOMAS KNUTSFORD (STOCKBRIDGE) HOUSE — 1753 —
PIGEON COVE, CAPE ANN, MASSACHUSETTS

The exterior of the house shows many additions to the original blockhouse; the first one was the ell to the north, which was probably built shortly after a transfer of the property in 1778, and is two and a half stories high with a stair hall and one room on each floor. The east end of the house was brought up to date during this alteration by the removal of the overhang at that end. The present owners installed the

of styles but give to it a picturesque outline and a feeling of having been lived in, which makes it very unusual among old houses.

In August, 1692, in the course of the witchcraft trials at Salem, John Procter and his wife, Elizabeth, were convicted and sentenced to be executed. He was hanged, but she, on account of pregnancy; was released on condition that she leave Salem. It is the tradition

Doorway, Garrison House Portion

Bay Window Added in Nineteenth Century

OLD GARRISON HOUSE (WITCH HOUSE), PIGEON COVE, CAPE ANN, MASSACHUSETTS

OLD GARRISON HOUSE (WITCH HOUSE), PIGEON COVE, CAPE ANN, MASSACHUSETTS

Dining Room End in North Wing Added in 1778

Southeast Living Room, Garrison House Part
WITCH HOUSE, PIGEON COVE, CAPE ANN, MASSACHUSETTS

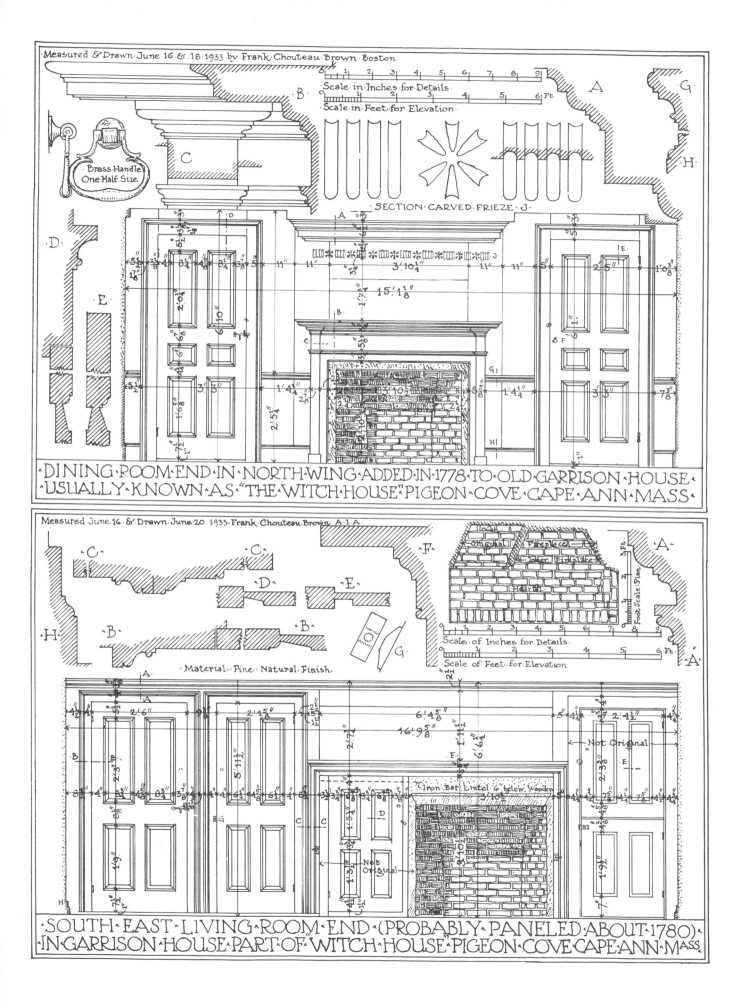

Measured & Drawn June 16 & 18 1933 by Frank Chouteau Brown Boston

Scale in Inches for Details

Scale in Feet for Elevation

Brass Handle One Half Size

SECTION CARVED FRIEZE J

·DINING·ROOM·END·IN·NORTH·WING·ADDED·IN·1778·TO·OLD·GARRISON·HOUSE·
·USUALLY·KNOWN·AS·"THE·WITCH·HOUSE"·PIGEON·COVE·CAPE·ANN·MASS·

Measured June 16 & Drawn June 20 1933 Frank Chouteau Brown A.I.A.

Original Fireplace
Later Fireplace
Hearth

Scale of Inches for Details

Scale of Feet for Elevation

·Material·Pine·Natural·Finish·

Not Original

Iron Bar Lintel 6" below Wooden

Not Original

·SOUTH·EAST·LIVING·ROOM·END·(PROBABLY·PANELED·ABOUT·1780)·
·IN·GARRISON·HOUSE·PART·OF·WITCH·HOUSE·PIGEON·COVE·CAPE·ANN·MASS·

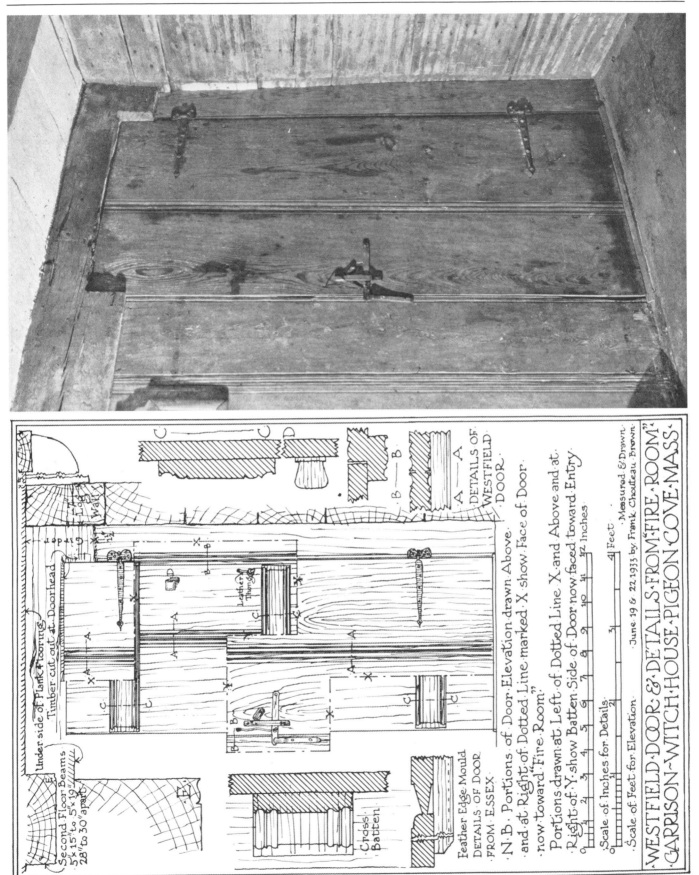

Feather Edge Mould
DETAILS OF DOOR
FROM ESSEX

N.B. Portions of Door Elevation drawn Above and at Right of Dotted Line marked X show Face of Door now toward "Fire Room"

Portions drawn at Left of Dotted Line X and Above and at Right of Y show Batten Side of Door now faced toward Entry

Scale of Inches for Details

Scale of Feet for Elevation.   June 19 & 22 1933 by Frank Chouteau Brown

WESTFIELD DOOR & DETAILS FROM "FIRE ROOM" GARRISON ~ WITCH HOUSE ~ PIGEON COVE ~ MASS.

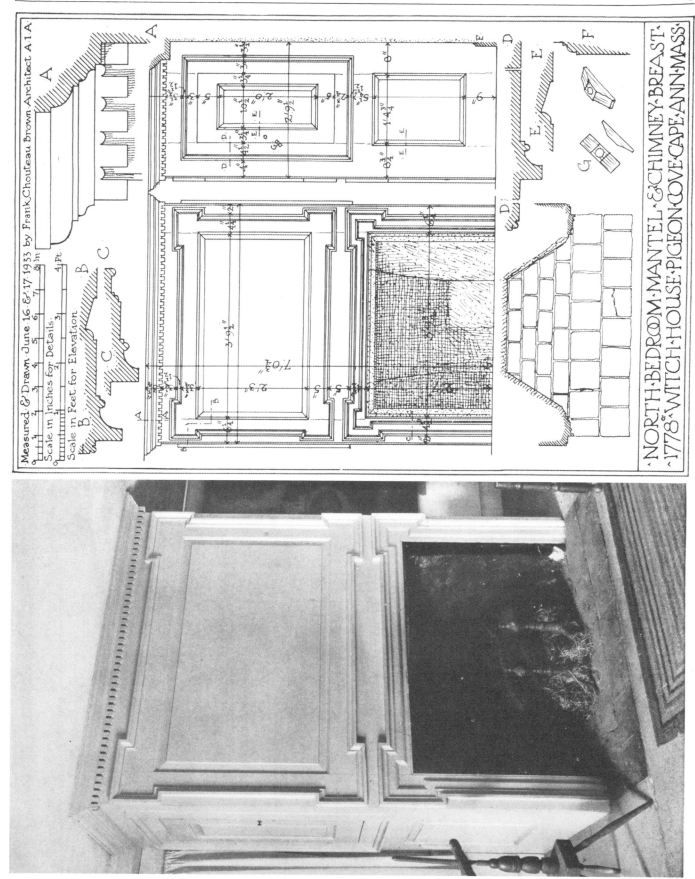

NORTH·BEDROOM·MANTEL·&·CHIMNEY·BREAST·
·1778·WITCH·HOUSE·PIGEON·COVE·CAPE·ANN·MASS·

Measured & Drawn June 16 & 17 1933 by Frank Chouteau Brown Architect A.I.A.

Scale in Inches for Details.

Scale in Feet for Elevation.

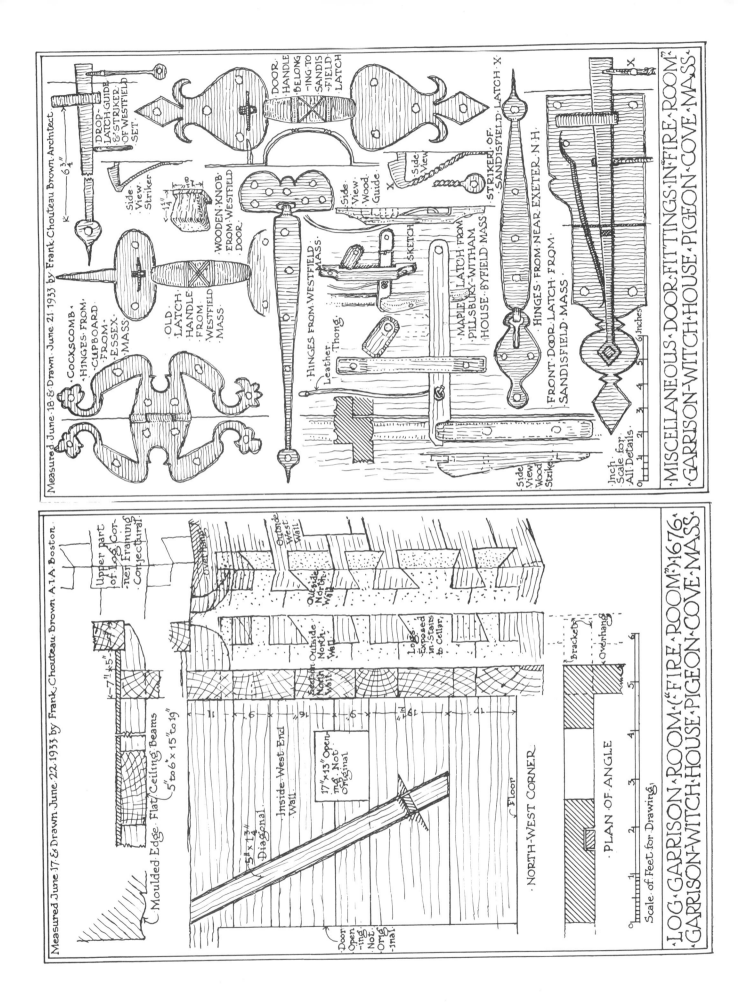

Measured June 18-8- Drawn June 21-1933 by Frank Chouteau Brown Architect.

K—6¾"—→

DROP·LATCH·GUIDE· &·STRIKER· OF·WESTFIELD SET·

Side View Striker

COCKSCOMB· HINGES·FROM· CLIPBOARD· FROM· ESSEX· MASS·

OLD· LATCH· HANDLE· FROM· WESTFIELD· MASS·

WOODEN·KNOB· FROM·WESTFIELD· DOOR·

DOOR· HANDLE· BELONG ·ING·TO· SANDIS ·FIELD· LATCH·

Side View Striker

HINGES·FROM·WESTFIELD· MASS·

Side·View· Wood· Guide·

SKETCH

Leather Thong

X

Side View Wood Guide

MAPLE·LATCH·FROM· PILLSBURY·WITHAM· HOUSE·BYFIELD·MASS·

STRIKER· OF· SANDISFIELD·LATCH· X·

HINGES·FROM·NEAR·EXETER·N·H·

FRONT·DOOR·LATCH·FROM· SANDISFIELD·MASS·

Side· View· Wood· Striker·

X

Inch· Scale·for· All·Details

0 1 2 3 4 5 6 Inches

·MISCELLANEOUS·DOOR·FITTINGS·IN·FIRE·ROOM? ·GARRISON·WITCH·HOUSE·PIGEON·COVE·MASS·

Measured June 17 & Drawn June 22·1933 by Frank Chouteau Brown A·I·A· Boston.

Upper part of Log Cor- ner Framing Conjectural·

Overhang

Outside West Wall

Outside North Wall

Section Outside North Wall

Logs Exposed in Stairs to Cellar·

K—7"×5"—→

"Moulded Edge· Flat Ceiling Beams 5" to 6" × 15" to 19"

11   6   16"   6   19½"   41

5"×13¼" Diagonal

Inside West End Wall

17"×13" Open- ing Not Original

Floor

·NORTH-WEST·CORNER·

Door Open- ing· Not· Orig- inal·

Bracket

Overhang

0 1 2 3 4 5 6
Scale· of· Feet· for· Drawing·

·PLAN·OF·ANGLE·

·LOG·GARRISON·ROOM· ("FIRE·ROOM")·1676· ·GARRISON·WITCH·HOUSE·PIGEON·COVE·MASS·

Living Room

WITCH HOUSE, PIGEON COVE, CAPE ANN, MASSACHUSETTS

THE CASTLE—1678—PIGEON COVE, MASSACHUSETTS

that her children gave her refuge in this house, hence the name Witch House which in recent years has been applied to it rather than the older and more appropriate one of The Garrison House.

Overlooking the south side of Pigeon Cove is The Castle, another weatherbeaten survivor of the earliest settlement of the North Village. Tradition ascribes to this house the date 1678, which is borne out by many details of its construction; the hewn overhang, the steep pitch and purlin construction of the roof, the heavy framing with deeply chamfered summer beams and "gunstock" posts, and the low ceilings.

This house, too, has changed with the times. Its chimney was rebuilt in the eighteenth century; rooms were plastered and paneled; a leanto was built, removed and rebuilt; all according to the changing tastes and fortunes of successive owners. Now, through the generosity of its last owners, the Story family, it has been presented to the Pigeon Cove Village Improve-

Fireplace in East Room

Fireplace in Living Hall
THE CASTLE—1678—PIGEON COVE, MASSACHUSETTS

ment Society, who have preserved and repaired it and hope eventually to furnish it appropriately. The kitchen has been restored to an approximation of what must have been its original appearance, while the parlor shows paneling and cased beams of the early eighteenth century, with a dado apparently made of moulded boards used originally for vertical sheathing.

The Gott House, on Halibut Point, the extreme point of the Cape, was built by Samuel Gott, who came from Wenham in 1702, and by whose descendants it is still owned and occupied. Probably the oldest gambrel-roofed house on the Cape, it offers an amusing example of a "jutby," that New England way of cutting a corner out of a house in the manner of a piece of cheese! The interior boasts two simple corner cupboards, but aside from that is unelaborated; one room-end sheathed, another paneled simply, the stair enclosed in a sheathed partition.

The Thomas Knutsford House was built in 1753 by Benjamin Stockbridge by whose name it is sometimes called. It faces south in the manner of early houses, away from the road, and is very attractive with its steep gambrel roof and tiny ell. It derives its name from Thomas Knutsford, Jr., a grandson of Stephen Knutsford and Mary Andrews, whose romance it recalls.

Mary Andrews was a beautiful and romantic girl who grew up in Pigeon Cove, and at the time of the Revolution was living, with her parents, in the woods near the shore. Given to day dreams, she fell in love with one of her visions, of whom she often dreamed; a handsome young man in uniform, who came from over the sea to be her husband. Sometimes in her dreams she conversed with him; they plighted their troth; then she would seem to see him lying injured on Andrews Point. She used to wander often to the spot, in hopes of finding him. But the years passed, and Mary Andrews seemed destined to remain a spinster. Until one day in 1778, wandering on Andrews Point she did find him there exhausted, lying with his head on his arm; young, handsome, in a British uniform! She revived him and brought him to her home; eventually he became her husband. A man of education and breeding, his origin was always clothed in mystery; whether because he was an escaped prisoner, a deserter, or whatever the reason, he never disclosed his story to his neighbors or communicated with his family. Their marriage was very happy, they had eight children and he taught school in the community until his death in 1807.

This community was poor and remote. These houses and many others of later date which still remain possess little elaboration either of plan or of architectural detail. Their scale, however, is almost invariably consistent and unbelievably small, with very low ceilings, doors of reduced size, and tiny details by which these small houses achieve a great measure of spaciousness and dignity. Built altogether of wood by men who had learned its qualities in building ships as well as houses, they show throughout a right use of this material. As we prepare to study the problem of the small house in the light of new materials and modern methods of production, let us learn what we can from these early solutions of a similar problem.

GOTT HOUSE—1702—HALIBUT POINT, PIGEON COVE, MASSACHUSETTS

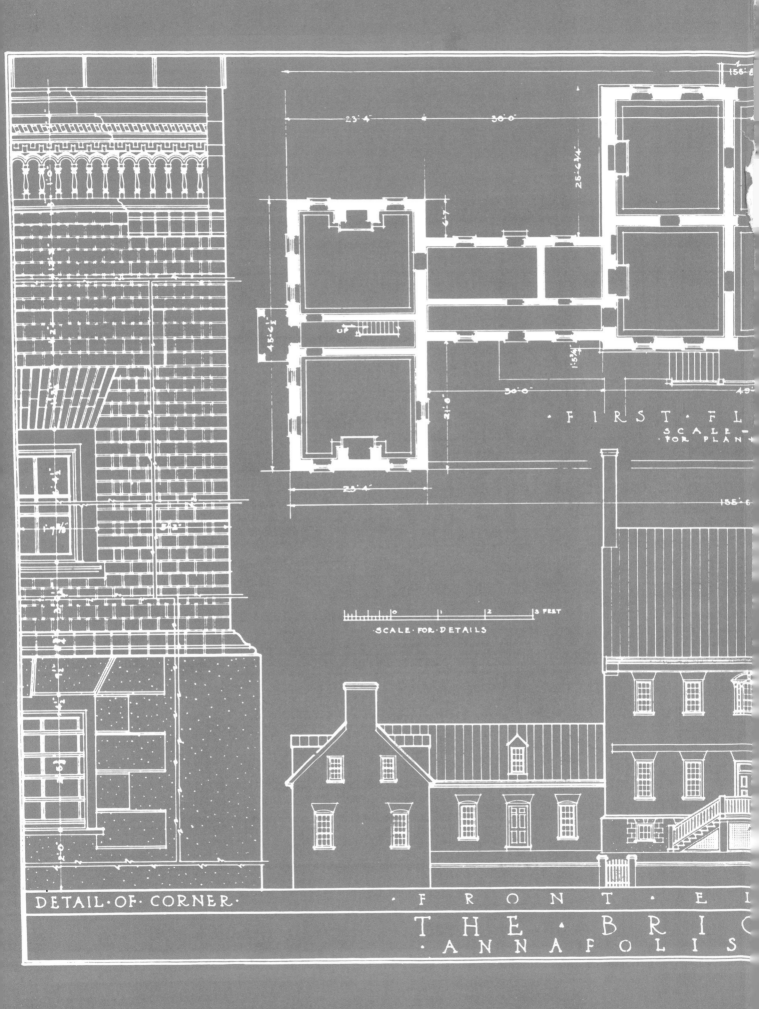

DETAIL·OF·CORNER·   ·F R O N T·E I

·FIRST·FL
SCALE·
FOR·PLAN

SCALE·FOR·DETAILS

T H E·B R I C
·A N N A P O L I S